HOW THE
SEC
BECAME
GOLIATH

THE MAKING OF COLLEGE FOOTBALL'S MOST DOMINANT CONFERENCE

RAY GLIER

HOWARD BOOKS
A Division of Simon & Schuster, Inc.
New York • Nashville • London • Toronto • Sydney • New Delhi

Howard Books
A Division of Simon & Schuster, Inc.
1230 Avenue of the Americas
New York, NY 10020

Copyright © 2012 by Ray Glier

First Howard Books hardcover edition September 2012

HOWARD and colophon are trademarks of Simon & Schuster, Inc.

For information about special discounts for bulk purchases,
please contact Simon & Schuster Special Sales at
1-866-506-1949 or business@simonandschuster.com.

The Simon & Schuster Speakers Bureau can bring authors to
your live event. For more information or to book an event,
contact the Simon & Schuster Speakers Bureau at
1-866-248-3049 or visit our website at www.simonspeakers.com.

Designed by Julie Schroeder

Manufactured in the United States of America

3   5   7   9   10   8   6   4   2

Library of Congress Cataloging-in-Publication Data

Glier, Ray.
How the SEC became goliath / Ray Glier.
p.   cm.
1. Southeastern Conference—History.
2. Football—Southern States—History.   I. Title.

GV958.5.S59G57 2012
796.332'630975—dc23   2012023927

ISBN 978-1-4767-0323-7
ISBN 978-1-4767-0328-2 (ebook)

For the sportswriters who lost their jobs in the recession.
Make your own way now.
Be entrepreneurs. I did it twenty years ago.

CONTENTS

INTRODUCTION

The national championship trophy has been in the South so long it has a sunburn. It is as much a fixture as the red, blue, and orange Solo cups that hold the tailgate drink and the $9.95 canvas-backed chair that holds the Southeastern Conference fan, who has no greater wish than to hold a winning lottery ticket and for his or her team to win on Saturday. The crystal Coaches' Trophy has bivouacked here since January 2007, and the folks who populate these rattlesnake-mean message boards in the South claim success comes from playing something called Big Boy Football.

Well, they might have a point. It is big-boy football, as in really big players playing the game. Big people beat up little people. That's what the SEC believes in; football that is played from the inside out, tackle to tackle, and coveting the defensive lineman over the wide receiver all day, every day. The Southeastern Conference has won six straight national championships in college football because it has size to go with speed.

Alabama and LSU of the SEC slugged it out for the national championship last January because they had 265-pound thumpers on defense that could scoot and 225-pound running backs that could plow. The 7-on-7 teams in the Big 12, ACC, Big East, and

Pac-10—the programs in those leagues that highlight skill players, not brawlers—sat home. Big people have become the prerequisite in the SEC, particularly at Alabama, which will not recruit runts for anything but kicker, and even then those specialists are ordered to muscle up. The success of the Crimson Tide, which won national titles in 2009 and 2011, and LSU, which has won 24 games the last two seasons and a title in 2007, should have spread-offense gurus rethinking their approach. Big and fast beats small and fast. It's why the SEC has not shared the road the last six seasons. It has big players who are fast, which is like a tractor trailer that rides down the middle of the highway stripe going 75 mph.

Bama uses an NFL-inspired formula to recruit. It wins from the inside out, which is with offensive and defensive linemen valued higher than wide receivers and quarterbacks. It builds muscle with a strenuous off-season program and finds high school recruits who can take tough coaching. Alabama takes the best athletes and puts them on defense, and NFL scouts have dubbed the Tide the thirty-third NFL franchise. LSU has the same rock-'em, sock-'em philosophy with Les Miles, the head coach; John Chavis, the defensive coordinator; and Greg Studrawa, the offensive coordinator. The Tigers hit you high where you live game after game after game and then run over you with cats such as the Honey Badger.

Now look at Auburn and Florida. Sure, they won national championships with some speed guys, and the SEC is known for fast players, but look closer. Who was really doing the heavy lifting for Auburn in 2010 and Florida in 2008? It was the Tigers' senior-laden offensive line making a path for the son of a preacher man, Cam Newton, who is 6-foot-6, 250 pounds. The other son of a preacher man, Tim Tebow, is 6-foot-3, 245 pounds, and built like a wishbone fullback, and he buckled defenses for important yards for the Gators in 2008 when they won the championship. Five players from that Florida offensive line that made the path easier for Jesus—that's what the O-line called Tebow—are playing or have played in the NFL. So take note of these numbers: Florida rushed for 231.1 yards per game in 2008. Auburn went for 284.8 yards a game in 2010. That is nice work in a defense-first establishment such as the SEC.

People always talk about the speed of the SEC. It's not just the speed. It's the size and the speed and the versatility of the offense and defense. That's why the SEC is Goliath. It has taken an imprint of the NFL and laid it over the top of its programs with NFL-type roster maestros called exactly what the NFL calls them: player personnel directors. Other conferences have personnel guys, but the SEC has personnel guys so skilled the NFL is hiring them. The Philadelphia Eagles plucked Ed Marynowitz off Alabama's staff in May 2012.

The SEC led the NFL draft with the most players selected for the sixth straight year, so maybe it is no coincidence it has won six straight championships. It was the only conference with a player selected from every one of its teams in 2012. Ohio State coach Urban Meyer, the former Florida coach, would tell people over and over when he was in Gainesville, "There are twelve teams in this league and ten of them think they can be big winners, so they pay their coaches and recruit like they are going to win the conference championship."

So for six straight years the SEC has walked off with the big crystal prize, and they will not give it back. The talk of Big Boy Football grinds on the Buckeyes, or Sooners, or Longhorns, or Ducks, and all they can come back with is "Wait until next year," and then next year comes and the SEC tribe is chanting in the closing minutes of the National Championship Game, "SEC, SEC, SEC," even if they are the only ones in the building.

Goliath gets the biggest prize and some of the biggest checks, too. In the last six seasons of the Bowl Championship Series, the SEC has cashed more than $150 million worth of checks from appearing in eleven BCS games. The BCS games and the revenue from its CBS/ESPN deals helped the conference pay out $20.1 million to each of its schools in 2012. Now that Missouri and Texas A&M have joined the conference, the deals with CBS and ESPN will be renegotiated to push distribution to each school probably toward $23 million. When the SEC finally gets around to launching its own network to provide content from its marquee hoops team, Kentucky, and its cavalcade of top ten baseball teams, the payout per school could reach $25 to $28 million, which means more money for coaches' salaries and recruiting and everything else that goes into keeping Goliath fed. Just add up the revenues pulled in by SEC schools. It's more than a billion dollars in receipts, more than any conference in the country.

The median athletics spending per athlete in the SEC in 2009 was $156,833. Per student in the SEC the median spending was $13,471, according to a study by the Delta Cost Project at the American Institutes for Research in Washington, DC. The median athletics spending per athlete in the Big 12 was $131,440 per athlete and $14,021 per student. In the ACC it was $106,238 for the athlete to $15,638 for the student. You look at those financials and wonder if the SEC has been a little too aggressive with the money grab. We'll examine Goliath's wallet in this book, too, right along with its Xs and Os.

Steve Berkowitz, who expertly investigates the finances of college athletics with a team of reporters for *USA Today*, simply says when explaining the SEC game of Monopoly with the national championship trophy, "Just follow the money."

Here is a snapshot of the money.

The vault for assistant coaches in college football, the area where many people thought the SEC lost all self-control, was opened up in 2009 by former Tennessee athletic director Mike Hamilton, who paid new head coach Lane Kiffin $2 million and paid Kiffin's father, defensive coordinator Monte Kiffin, $1.2 million. Recruiting coordinator and offensive line coach Ed Orgeron was knocking down $650,000, and offensive coordinator and line coach Jim Chaney received $380,000. The arms race in college football had entered a new era with these assistants' salaries, and the SEC was out in front.

The former Florida offensive coordinator Charlie Weis signed a three-year contract that paid him $765,000 in 2011 and would have paid him $865,000 in 2012 and 2013 if he had not accepted the head coaching job at Kansas. Weis's salary at the time was higher than that of forty-one Division I head coaches, according to data compiled by *USA Today*.

It was a pittance compared to the deal offensive coordinator Gus Malzahn had at Auburn before he left to become the head coach at Arkansas State. He was drawing $1.3 million per year to coach one side of the ball in 2010. John Chavis, the LSU defensive coordinator, will eventually make $1.1 million a season as his deal matures. Kirby Smart, the defensive coordinator at Alabama, is making $950,000.

Some strength and conditioning coaches in the SEC are making $300,000 and more. SEC schools do not talk about all the personnel they have hired in the last five years in football, but some staffs have as many as twelve people devoted to strength and conditioning. It really is an arms—and legs—race in the SEC.

"Two significant areas of spending escalation have been in salaries paid to football personnel, head and assistant football coaches, and an increasing number of noncoaching staff, such as strength and conditioning personnel and directors of recruiting, video services, player development, etc.," said Amy Perko, the executive director of the Knight Commission on Intercollegiate Athletics. "SEC teams have been pacesetters in each of these areas. Big-time college football is like a high-stakes poker game, with the SEC upping the ante every year.

"The impact of the escalation is of great concern to presidents, who are also pessimistic about their ability to control these costs on their own campuses."

So the SEC wins with big people who can run, but it also wins with an aggressive hunting of cash. Perko is correct. No conference is more responsible for escalating the arms race in college athletics in facilities and coaches' contracts than the SEC. The presidents of the schools in the SEC have been pushed and pushed to win in football by millions of fans in the South, and now the rest of college football has taken up the chase with expansion, their own mega–TV deals, and coaches' contracts. Iowa's Kirk Ferentz, once the lone $3-million-a-year coach in the Big Ten, finally has some companions in the vault in Ohio State coach Urban Meyer ($4 million) and Michigan coach Brady Hoke ($3.2 million average over six years). The man the SEC has to worry about is the Pac-12 commissioner, Larry Scott, whose aggressive business deals are tripling the cash payouts to Pac-12 schools, which means more money to sign the best assistant coaches and build out facilities.

The SEC cash also provides for recruiting budgets. When the select SEC head coach says he is going recruiting for a week, it does not mean he is packing a suitcase and will be on the road enduring bedbugs and punch-drunk hotel clerks. Alabama, for instance, has a jet at the disposal of its head coach, just like a lot of other SEC coaches have. It takes the coach from town to town in the South. Most of the time he is back at night sleeping in his own bed.

The assistants, on the other hand, will drive miles and miles after spring practice in late April, from north Alabama to Florida. They can get on a jet, too, and be dropped off one by one in different locales, then be picked up one by one, but they also endure plenty of windshield time with the sixteen-hour days by car as they roll from school to school to school in their recruiting area.

Auburn's head coach, Gene Chizik, and his assistant coaches traveled the state of Alabama in limousines to recruit. The former Tennessee coach Kiffin hopped around Atlanta one Friday night in a helicopter watching several high school games his prospects were playing in. Presidents are not the only luminaries skipping over traffic jams in copters.

The zeal and competitiveness in the South is why college football is thick with the acrimony, SEC vs. Everyone Else. The other conferences cannot match the fervor for football in the South. It is why the SEC fought the four-team play-off format that allowed only conference champions into the postseason. The rest of college football dreads the idea of another all-SEC National Championship Game because the second-place SEC team can be better than the other guy's first-place team. So when will the rest of college football chase down the SEC?

Lane Kiffin, who coached a season at Tennessee, is making his way up the rankings at Southern Cal and has already proved he is more than a brash kid with a whistle; that he can call plays and rebuild a brand. Urban Meyer, the former Florida coach, is off to a great start at Ohio State. He is making enemies with his recruiting style. Now, that's more like the SEC, which is the king of aggressive recruiting.

Jimbo Fisher, who comes off the Saban coaching tree, is refilling the tank at Florida State. He understands he is not competing with the ACC. He is competing with the SEC and pouring himself into the job like an SEC coach. Clemson is paying its offensive coordinator, Chad Morris, $1.3 million, which is in the style of the SEC.

The SEC should fear Kiffin, Meyer, and Fisher because they have seen the SEC up close. They are ardent recruiters and have sharp-minded staffs. All three can dominate their conferences and get into the National Championship Game, but their schools still don't have quite enough loot, like the SEC, to sign up the top assistant coaches. Clemson chased LSU's Chavis to be defensive coordinator, but could not outbid the Tigers in money or prestige or access to top players.

How did it all become so galvanized for the SEC?

Well, this book is not a celebration of the Southeastern Conference's golden era and six milestones. It is about the passage to those titles. I'm not rooting for anybody in this book, just trying to explain a few things, from the SEC's perspective, of course. Losers don't write the history books.

The story does not start with Florida's bludgeoning of Ohio State, 41–14, on January 8, 2007, which was the first title in the SEC six-pack. It has to start with the population quake in certain southern states—Georgia, South Carolina, Florida—which helps account for a deep pool of high school talent for SEC teams to choose from. Texas A&M and Missouri joined the SEC on July 1, 2012, which adds another ripple of muscle to the SEC footprint.

The story has to include the migration of black athletes from baseball to football in the 1970s and 1980s. The eighty-five scholarships offered by a Division I program and the allure of adoring crowds on Saturday sure beat a bus ride to Bristol, Tennessee, or a frosty college baseball game played in late February. The SEC story includes the bold move to include a conference championship game twenty years ago, which has given the SEC champion a boost toward the BCS title game.

The SEC success story has to talk about Mobile, Alabama, the baseball home of Hank Aaron, Satchel Paige, Billy Williams, Willie McCovey, and Ozzie Smith, among others, and how that southern city has turned into a stronghold of football with first-round picks such as Auburn defensive lineman Nick Fairley, LSU quarterback JaMarcus Russell, Alabama safety Mark Barron, and on and on.

This book offers a good dose of Nick Saban, but it does not start with Saban's first contribution to the title streak, his 2009 championship team at Alabama. It starts with his 2001 recruiting class at LSU, which awakened an on-again, off-again program and led to the 2003 LSU title and then the 2007 championship. The Tigers have been on an eleven-year roll. The deliberate Saban then did for Alabama (2009, 2011) what he did for LSU.

The dominance of the SEC has a lot more to do with the South's culture than just the rock-'em, sock-'em of football played one day a week. The South lost the Civil War, and sociologists will tell you that there is still a regional angst and an "us against them," a spirit of "those damn Yankees," 147 years following the end of the war.

While white players are more wrapped up in the mythological aspect—win one for the South—black players see opportunity in the game, and a chance to shine in their communities. The cult of SEC football gets at the consciousness of the South, and that has to be part of this book. What it means to be a man and tough.

So, do you write this book and have to hold your nose at the same time? Did the SEC get here by kicking the dog, being home wreckers, crashing their motorcycles, behaving as general badasses, and cheating? I thought about that. According to the NCAA Major Infractions database, the SEC has had eight major infractions in football since 2002, which was just before it started building rosters for this six-year run. There were many other secondary violations, which the conference office and schools do their best to keep from public view. It sounded as if the SEC should not be in jail, but under it.

I looked at the recent college football scandal sheet: North Carolina, Miami, Ohio State, Boise State, Oregon, and Penn State. A couple of years ago it was Michigan and Southern California.

Also, since 2002, the Pac-12 has had eight major infractions. The Atlantic Coast Conference had five. The Big 12 and Big Ten have had four each. The NCAA bill has not come due for Oregon and its relationship with player broker Willie Lyles, but when it does, the Pac-12 will be the clubhouse leader with nine major infractions since 2002.

When Yahoo! or the *New York Times* look under rocks, do they find just the SEC slithering away? Hardly. Many schools have loopholes and shortcuts written in the margins of their NCAA manual. Let's get that squared away right now. The SEC has not won six titles by outcheating people. The other conferences can't run that rap on the SEC.

But they try.

Right after Alabama defeated LSU in the all-SEC National Championship Game, John Cooper, the former Ohio State football coach (1988–2000), told a Cleveland radio station, according to the *Birmingham News*:

I see some of these teams, the Auburns. I'm told, I don't know and I haven't coached in that league, but I'm told that down South the Alabamas and LSUs and some of these teams that have these great players, that maybe the NCAA needs to look into their situation. Those teams have been on probation. As you know, Alabama's certainly one of the most penalized teams in college football, as is the Southeastern Conference. We say the SEC's the best and they are the best, but they've also had more NCAA violations than probably all the other leagues put together the last ten years.

That is not true, but it is part of the perception of the SEC. Since 2002, the SEC has had eight major violations. The Big 12, Pac-12, Big Ten, and ACC had twenty-one combined, soon to be twenty-two with Oregon's mess. Do the math, Coop.

In March, after the NCAA sentenced North Carolina's football program to a one-year bowl ban and other sanctions for nine violations, former Carolina safety Deunta Williams told the *Raleigh (NC) News & Observer*, "What happened at Carolina is child's play compared to what happens at the SEC. The SEC pays for players. I'm not afraid to say it, but the NCAA doesn't go after them."

He offered no examples of infractions to chase down. I tried to contact him. In August 2011, I was in Chapel Hill, and athletes in other sports talked about a glistening SUV driven by a Carolina defensive lineman who was bumping to the machine's music while cruising through campus. That's child's play? How about the academic cheating at Carolina and Florida State? More child's play, I suppose.

Consider the two southern schools that prevented the SEC from a greater haul of titles ten to fifteen years ago. They cheated. Florida

State and Miami have been pushed into the margins of the game by scandals, and they have had to deal with the fallout, which was to lose a few games and push aside an icon (Bobby Bowden).

"It's stupid to say everyone is doing it, and it's stupid to say only the SEC is doing it," said Mike Oriard, former player at Notre Dame, retired professor at Oregon State, and author of *Bowled Over*, a book on the culture of college football.

It is true that when Alabama and LSU played the National Championship Game in January 2012, both schools were still on probation for NCAA violations in football. That had to be a first. You know the old taunt: SEC stands for Surely Everyone's Cheating. The SEC has its issues, no question about it. Alabama banned a clothing salesman from its sidelines because memorabilia signed by players was showing up in his store with price tags. LSU fired an assistant coach for improper recruiting. And you know about Cam Newton's father, Cecil, who was shopping Auburn's former quarterback down the SEC aisle at Mississippi State.

Fans of rival conferences want to read about the dark secrets of the SEC. The business of the SEC does look shameless with the coaching contracts, the stadiums stuffed with blind, obedient revelers, the decaying classroom across the street from the modern locker room, the polished steel in the weight rooms, the manipulation of academics, and the oversigning and the managing of rosters, as if the NFL had been transplanted to the SEC. The resources that go into the cultivation of an SEC football program are mind-bending, and rival conferences claim overindulgence 24-7.

But if you look at the bank account of an Ohio State, can you really accuse the SEC of buying titles? If all it took was money, the Buckeyes ($131 million athletic department budget) would have interrupted this SEC run by now. What about Texas, the last non-SEC team to win the national championship ($150 million in revenue)?

That has not stopped the sniping. Wisconsin coach Bret Bielema told the *Sporting News*, "We at the Big Ten don't want to be like the SEC in any way, shape, or form."

The Big Ten is *not* like the SEC in any way, shape, or form. The crystal trophies on SEC campuses attest to that. More proof is the Big Ten's 1-10 record versus the SEC in bowl games. The Big Ten was also the conference that rode Maurice Clarett to its last national championship. Everyone remembers the Ohio State running back. Jailed for armed robbery. Given preferential treatment by a professor at Ohio State, and on and on. How does Bielema claim overindulgence by the SEC when the other quarterbacks in his program, slaving through off-season workouts, were pushed aside by the one-year hire of quarterback Russell Wilson? Sure, Auburn hired a quarterback (Cam Newton) for a season, but the Tigers did not turn around and act sanctimonious toward other programs. They also thought they would have Newton two years.

So what don't we see? What's in this book that also speaks to the essence of the SEC?

• Nick Saban walking across the hot coals of mistrust in south Baton Rouge to recruit a star to help awaken LSU.

• The SEC schools that petition the conference office to allow the school to remove a player from the roster and its scholarship count for medical reasons and the conference office saying, "No, you can't do this. Kids are not disposable. You have to prove it."

• The Tennessee athletic department members e-mailing athletic director Mike Hamilton pleading for him to corral Lane Kiffin, who was trying to cut in line in the SEC's championship parade with questionable tactics. Kiffin was tearing down some traditions at Tennessee, and it was good for him that he made a quick exit because former players were about fed up.

• The private eyes on the SEC looking for rule-bending or rule-breaking so they could shake down the league and slow down the SEC's dominance. For example, it was a booster from a Big 12 school who called the NCAA and said a former NFL star was recruiting Foley, Alabama, star Julio Jones for his alma mater, which is Alabama. The former star explained it as innocent contact and the NCAA dismissed it.

What else about the SEC do we have to see to explain this six-year run?

• Urban Meyer walking with his head down in the darkened tunnel at Bryant-Denny Stadium, his spread offense humiliated by Alabama on October 1, 2005, 31–3, while reporters trashed his scheme up in the press box. The determined Meyer didn't punt; he won a title in 2006 with big-back adjustments to the spread—and a ferocious defense. Meyer then recruited the ultimate spread quarterback, Tim Tebow, and won another championship in 2008 with one of the best teams in the history of college football.

• How two missed field goals by an NFL-caliber kicker in a non-SEC game—Pitt vs. West Virginia—helped determine the SEC's fate in 2007. Pitt stunned West Virginia 13–9 in that game to open the door for LSU to win the 2007 title. The season before, UCLA stunned Southern California 13–9 to open the door for Florida. Luck happens even for the mighty SEC.

• The coach who turned down LSU and its head coaching offer in November 1999, which opened the door for the Tigers to hire Nick Saban. The hiring of Saban helped the SEC achieve the status it enjoys today in college football.

Sure, there are excesses in SEC football. You can't alibi those away. You cannot cover your eyes to the oversigning of recruits, which the SEC office and decent athletic directors such as Georgia's Greg McGarity finally had to step in and stop. Some coaches fought against the oversigning legislation and lost. The official vote by schools to put in some checks against oversigning was reported as 12–0, but that was polish at the end of contentious meetings, which did not start with a 12–0 vote. One reason SEC coaches were signing more than twenty-five high school players per year to scholarships was because they were handing out scholarships to kids with risky academic backgrounds. The coaches didn't know if the high school senior was going to qualify academically, and the coaches wanted to be covered with an extra recruit, or two, or five. The second reason is they wanted some extra players ready to step in when they ran off players who were underperforming or not holding up their end of the scholarship bargain by skipping class or getting busted for marijuana use.

The SEC office has lately been active in policing the integrity of the conference, but that has not stopped some from outside the SEC from wondering how certain players get on the field for SEC teams. A coach from the Southwestern Athletic Conference, which includes schools such as Grambling State and Alcorn State, once lamented to an NFL scout about a player at an SEC school, "We couldn't get him in here. How did they get him in there?"

To be clear, the SEC follows the minimum NCAA academic guidelines for admitting athletes. Besides, if it was so automatic to get into SEC schools, would there be so many prospects tucked away in prep school or junior college?

Plenty of barbs have been heaved at the SEC during this six-year stretch of championships, but it is important to consider one statistic. In the second annual "Adjusted Graduation Gap Report" done by the College Sport Research Institute (CCRI) at the University of North Carolina, SEC schools graduated football players 18 percent less than the general full-time student body (2000–03 four-class cohort). That's nothing to be proud of, except when it is put side by side with other conferences, the conferences that claim the SEC is a den of cheaters. The Big Ten, which has created the biggest stink about SEC football and academics, graduated football players 21 percent less than the general full-time student body. The Atlantic Coast Conference graduated athletes 20 percent less. The Pac-12 was last among Division I conferences, graduating players at 26 percent less than the full-time student body. The SEC has more restraint when it comes to athletics vis-à-vis academics than other conferences would want you to believe.

Perhaps we should consider the background of some of the football players who are signed into the SEC. The city of Atlanta, Georgia, public schools are dealing with one of the worst cases of standardized-test cheating in the history of US education. Put your kid in one of these deplorable public school systems in the South and see how he turns out. Why not give a kid free access to tutors, paid for by the athletic department, and see what he does with the opportunity? The players pour money into the pockets of the professional sports managers in the conferences, but SEC schools do put a significant amount of money back into tutoring programs in the SEC, and that's a good thing.

There is a trend in Division I athletics for schools to hire learning specialists to work with the low-functioning football/basketball players when they get on campus. My contention is that this is exactly what universities should be expected to do. That football money is being used for learning specialists is more than appropriate. Cynics might say it is merely to keep kids eligible for the next game, and that certainly has something to do with it. But legitimate students are on the two-deep, more than you think, who take advantage of the extra help and thrive. Maybe these bloggers should walk on campus, stop a player, and ask about the tutoring and its value. Dig a little. Sniping is easy.

Most of the schools in the SEC are land-grant institutions. They were established to educate the masses, not the elite. They are not supposed to be overly selective, and, yes, SEC schools have academic entrance requirements so that high school players who can only fog a piece of glass are not routinely given scholarships.

You can count on one hand the BCS schools who have remained 100 percent true to the mission of academics first. Northwestern, Stanford, Duke, Vanderbilt. The back door to the admissions office is usually locked at those schools. They pay the most attention to the twenty-hour rule for athletes, which is a joke in the SEC. Football is a full-time job in the SEC—forty hours a week—but it's that way at a lot of schools in other conferences, and it's that way in baseball, swimming, volleyball, soccer, and some country-club sports, too.

Mark Emmert, the president of the NCAA, who is spearheading new academic guidelines for athletics, toasts the SEC and its run of titles. The man who hired Nick Saban at LSU did not swipe at Goliath over academics versus football.

"I think it's a pretty remarkable run," he said. "If the universities are using that success to advance their academic agenda, then it's a great thing. What's to be unhappy about that? From our experience at LSU, we were able to elevate academics and athletics simultaneously."

But the reporter's task is to get as close to the truth as possible and ask, "Is there more?"

There is more. It is not just about buying championships. The SEC is about culture, climate, and competitiveness.

It is about players.

Six of the top ten states with the most players in the NFL, per capita, are within the SEC footprint, according to former Dallas Cowboys executive and NFL.com analyst Gil Brandt. You won't believe which state ranks first in players per capita in the SEC. You won't believe which state ranks second. The SEC states not only have more players, they have better players where it counts in today's game of the quarterback-centric spread offense: defensive linemen.

The SEC produces more NFL defensive linemen than any other BCS league, and that is a big deal as the game, in other conferences and the NFL, shifts more and more into the hands of the quarterback. Defenses win by affecting the quarterback, not just with sacks, but with pressures, and SEC defenses are good at sending marauders, such as Alabama's Marcell Dareus, LSU's Glenn Dorsey, and Florida's Derrick Harvey, at the quarterback. Ask Ohio State,

Oregon, and Texas, all losers to the SEC in the National Championship Game, about the pressure created by the SEC defensive fronts.

It is about coaches.

In six seasons at Florida, Urban Meyer was 65-15. In five seasons at Alabama, Nick Saban is 50-12. In seven seasons at LSU, Les Miles is 75-17. In eleven seasons at Georgia, Mark Richt is 106-38. In seven seasons at South Carolina, Steve Spurrier is 55-35. No other BCS conference could roll out more accomplished coaches in the six-year title streak.

We might not hit every note in this book, but at least we are going to give you something else to consider besides the SEC's fat wallet.

Once upon a time, Johnny Majors, the Tennessee football coach and former Vols all-American, shook his head from side to side in despair and declared in his raspy voice that the SEC was too good for its own good. It was 1989 and Auburn had defensive linemen of freakish size and speed, Tennessee was stamping out NFL-caliber receivers and running backs, Alabama was about to flex its muscle again with Gene Stallings in 1990, and Florida had just hired an inventive coach named Steve Spurrier. The SEC was in the middle of an eleven-season run (1981 to 1991) without winning a national title, and Majors said it had to do with the fierceness of conference play.

"We beat each other up too much now," Majors said. "An SEC team can't win a national championship."

He was wrong, of course. Six times wrong in the last six years.

CHAPTER 1

THE EARLY SEC

Eighty years ago, the SEC did not have an issue with student-athletes transferring here and there, but it had trouble with *migrants*. The SEC did not have to unearth scandals about players being paid, but there were investigations of players being *subsidized*. There were no issues with alumni providing extra benefits to players, but there was a problem with scholarships being provided under *unauthorized programs*. There was no issue with ineligible players, but there was an issue with *tramp athletes*.

You don't recognize the language? It's all the same, of course. The issues today with college football were the same issues in 1932 when the SEC was formed; there were just different labels put on misdeeds. Transfers were migrants. Subsidies were illegal payoffs. Unauthorized programs were more illegal payoffs. Tramp athletes were ineligible players, hired hands who came out of the hills September to November, then went home after the final whistle.

Your ears are filled up today with the high jinks of college football and the expansion of conferences and the money grab. This is new? You think there are problems now with bad actors in college football and conference realignment and schools looking for the best deal? The same issues that existed a hundred years ago continue to spill over into the academic side of campus today.

———

In fact, the insults to the academic mission of universities nationally are nothing compared to what happened a hundred years ago. Some players in the 1890s played for three or four schools. Some college football players didn't even attend the college they played for, according to author John D. McCallum, who wrote *Southeastern Conference Football: America's Most Competitive Conference.*

You think fourteen is too many schools for one conference? How about twenty-three schools in one league?

Try blaming TV for that. There was no TV.

The evolution of the SEC and other conferences has come a long way, but it has also gone nowhere. The issues of 1932 are still the issues of today. You resist a focus on the negative—the recruiting, the paying of players, eligibility issues—in a great game such as college football, but that is why the conference office and the office of the commissioner were created in the first place: oversight and regulation. Considering the severity of issues eighty years ago, the conference office has done a credible job cleaning up college football. At least, I don't think there are any more *tramp athletes.*

So who had the bright idea to corral college athletics a hundred years ago? Just the people who should have had the idea. The teachers. It was not athletic directors and presidents who organized the first response to the controversies and quarrels in college athletics, it was faculty. There were no athletic directors, and coaches were part-time employees at some schools. Presidents had a university to operate and football was not a major budget concern. Imagine that.

So when a meeting was convened at the Kimball House, a hotel in downtown Atlanta, on December 22, 1894, to address concerns about athletics on some southern campuses, it was a chemistry professor, Dr. William L. Dudley, who led the meeting of faculty representatives. The faculty reps had worries about the campus-wide emphases on college football and other intercollegiate sports.

Sound familiar?

Dudley was from Vanderbilt, which is still regarded as the most pure academically among SEC schools. The other schools with representatives present were Alabama Polytechnic Institute, Georgia School of Technology, University of Alabama, University of Georgia, University of North Carolina, and the University of the South. They created the SIAA, the Southern Intercollegiate Athletic Association, which did not have enforcement power and was largely impotent, but it served a significant purpose.

The faculty reps set some guidelines, even though they could not penalize programs. There were to be no players who were not students at the school where they played. They could not play under assumed names and could not receive gifts to play for a particular school. Students who were failing classes could not play in the games, and the college teams could not play professional teams. The SIAA barred coaches from playing, which had been standard practice.

"It got a foundation in place," said Andy Doyle, an associate professor of history at Winthrop University, who specializes in southern history and is a native of Birmingham, Alabama. "It got schools accustomed to there being some sort of sanctioning body; it brought people around to accepting the notion that ceding some sort of university autonomy was a necessary part of creating a functioning system of competition.

"The early conferences had very little authority because the schools do not want to concede power to any administrative body, but the conferences gradually accumulated enforcement power."

Soon after it was formed, the SIAA immediately attempted to apply some handcuffs to the overreaching of players and coaches. It requested that schools limit participation to five years, prohibited pay to athletes, and said "migratory" athletes had to remain in residence for a year before they could play, which is exactly the stipulation that exists today regarding transfers. There were no birds of flight from one school to the next. The SIAA was the first conference for the South, the early forerunner of today's SEC, whose office is located on Twenty-Second Street in downtown Birmingham, Alabama. It all started in that hotel in Atlanta, which has since been demolished.

The early faculty representatives of the SIAA did not hover over football as much as they did baseball. The exact phrase used in their early work was to "correct the evils of baseball," according to Melvin Henry Gruensfelder, whose thesis in 1964 for the University of Illinois was "A History of the Origin and Development of the Southeastern Conference." Imagine that, a Big Ten scholar writing on the history of the SEC. The thick, hardbound copy of the thesis is in the archives of the SEC office in Birmingham. In 1895, twelve more schools sent faculty representatives to an SIAA meeting, and membership eventually reached thirty schools. It was the original Super Conference.

But something more cultural, more deeply rooted to the South led to the creation of a conference of schools. Doyle said the new southern man wanted to be seen as an equal to the northern man. The Civil War had crushed the ego of the South. The North was more urbanized and industrialized. It's why the North won the war, and the South wanted to raise the level of its game, so to speak. Football was part of the formula.

"In the 1880s a new generation of southerners, white southerners, want to urbanize, industrialize, basically create the same bourgeoisie capitalism system in the South that existed in the North, which was one of the primary reasons the Confederates lost the Civil War," Doyle said. "Football was a part of this. Football was an elite sport. It was played by university students when less than five percent of that age cohort [eighteen to twenty-two] went to college.

"It was the way of defining yourself as elite, and more especially for southerners, it was a way of identifying with the most progressive elements in the North."

The whole concept was labeled *elite regeneration*, and the South dove headfirst into football to get even with the North. Nothing could turn back the southern surge for the game, not even tragedy.

In 1897, a University of Georgia player, Richard Von Gammon, suffered a fatal head injury in a game against Virginia. Georgia lawmakers passed a bill that made playing football a criminal offense punishable by a year on the chain gang. Governor William Yates Atkinson vetoed the measure following a plea from Von Gammon's mother (she did not want the sport banned because her son loved the game), but that wasn't all there was to Atkinson's veto. Doyle said Atkinson's message in his veto also included, "What will the Yankees think of us?" Doyle said Atkinson vetoed the bill because of southern pride as much as anything else. If the South could not navigate through a controversy presented by football, the Yankees might think the southerners inept and a bunch of rubes. After all, the North had seen tragedy from football, particularly at the hands of the brutal "flying wedge," and the North was still playing the game.

Dudley, whom Doyle described as a decent and honorable man,

believed in Walter Camp's creed that football could build a better man. Camp, a coach at Yale and considered the father of American football, defined football as a way of training executives and building leadership abilities. That is exactly what Dudley wanted for the South's new generation of leaders.

The creation of the SIAA, Doyle said, was also part of Dudley's personal crusade to enforce the ideals of amateur competition. "He truly believed in what he was doing," Doyle said.

In January 1895, three weeks after the SIAA meeting in Atlanta, at a meeting in the Palmer House in Chicago, the Big Ten was born. Called the Western Conference, it had seven members: the University of Chicago, University of Illinois, University of Michigan, University of Minnesota, Northwestern University, Purdue University, and the University of Wisconsin. Indiana University and the State University of Iowa were admitted in 1899.

While SIAA had its first organizational meeting the month before the Western Conference schools, Doyle said the SIAA is not regarded as the first "official" conference because its schools were not willing to cede authority like the schools in the Western Conference.

The Big Ten, which currently has twelve members, had nine members at the turn of the century. The Big Ten started with its own ideals and goals on how to corral big-time athletics: freshmen and graduate students were not allowed to play. There were no training tables, or meal tables, for athletes. Coaches were appointed by the schools, and according to the Big Ten website, they were appointed "at modest salaries."

The Big Ten created an office of the commissioner in 1922, and it has been quite stable. There have been just five commissioners of the Big Ten. The current commissioner, Jim Delany, has held the office since 1989 and has taken personal responsibility in trying to keep the SEC honest in football. Delany has also brought the Big Ten its windfall of money with the Big Network, which has almost evened the playing field with the SEC in money to pay coaches, among other benefits.

The Pac-12 has its roots back to 1959, but was then called the Athletic Association of Western Universities (AAWU). For years it was the Pac-8, then it became the Pac-10 in 1978 when it added Arizona and Arizona State. Now with the addition of Colorado and Utah, it is the Pac-12. Its flagship football team through the years has been the University of Southern California.

The Pac-12's key figure is currently businessman Larry Scott, the commissioner, who has reeled in money for the SEC with TV and marketing deals. It used to be the western schools had to make up for their athletic departments' deficits to play sports, but Scott's leadership in TV deals is making more Pac-12 schools self-sufficient.

The most shamed conference was the old Southwest Conference because Southern Methodist University was hit by the NCAA's death penalty in 1987 and had its football program shut down. The SWC was one of the oldest athletic conferences in college sports, created on December 8, 1914, in Houston. The charter members of the conference were Baylor, Oklahoma A&M (Oklahoma State), Rice, Southwestern University, Texas A&M, Texas, Arkansas, and Oklahoma.

The SWC lasted until 1996, finally blown apart by NCAA scandals and realignment. Some members went to the Big 12, which was officially formed in 1996.

The SEC actually had a hand in the creation of the Big 12. When Roy Kramer, the commissioner of the SEC, took the SEC into a contract with CBS, it essentially ruined the television pact of the College Football Association, which had included the SEC, Big Eight, and

Southwest Conference. When the SEC left, the Big Eight and Southwest Conference started exploring a joint deal in 1994 with ABC. Negotiations moved along, and Texas debated joining the Pac-10. Finally, four Southwest Conference schools—Texas, Texas A&M, Baylor, and Texas Tech—joined the Big Eight to create the Big 12.

Colorado has since left the Big 12 to join the Pac-10, and Nebraska left the Big 12 to join the Big Ten, and the Big 12 went to ten teams. It went back to twelve teams in July 2012 with the addition of West Virginia and TCU. Got all that?

Realignment is nothing new in college athletics, but the era eighty years ago and today are distinct. While football and television money drives all realignment now, baseball, geography, and freshman eligibility had the biggest impact on schools' partnering up one hundred, ninety, and eighty years ago. The other issue in realignments back in the day was what to do with the tramp athlete, the big, countryside farm laborer who arrived for the start of the season in September and left right after the Thanksgiving Day game, the last contest of the season. He was not there to attend class; just win games. Many cynics today claim the practice continues on the modern campus, with players stringing along a class schedule just long enough to get trained up and eligible for the NFL.

One of the earliest issues that broke apart confederations of schools was the "one-year rule." Smaller schools said they could not compete with bigger schools and wanted their freshmen eligible so they could have a greater number of players, according to Gruensfelder. The big schools in the South back in the early 1900s had just five hundred to six hundred students, while the smaller schools had two hundred students.

At a December 1920 meeting of the Southern Intercollegiate Athletic Association, some of the larger schools, Alabama, Kentucky, and North Carolina, among others, proposed a rule change making freshmen ineligible. Another issue was a workable schedule, with schools scattered so far apart, but the real issue, freshman eligibility, was more thorny. In a vote, the big schools were defeated. Freshmen could play. The big schools broke away, but they did not have to wait long to find a new home.

In a February 25–26, 1921, meeting in Atlanta, fourteen former members from the SIAA formed the Southern Conference. These were Alabama, Auburn, Clemson, Georgia, Georgia Tech, Kentucky, Maryland, Mississippi State, North Carolina, North Carolina State, Tennessee, Virginia, Virginia Tech, and Washington and Lee. Dr. S. V. Sanford of Georgia was made acting chairman.

Six more schools were added in 1922. Three more schools were added between 1923 and 1929, and the Southern Conference swelled to twenty-three members. During this time, public interest in college athletics swept the country in an improved post–World War I economy. The faculty representatives were starting to lose some of their control as the sport grew more popular.

"In the midst of the dilemma stood the faculty representative and the organization he created to extend his control—the athletic association," wrote Gruensfelder. "His primary purpose was to keep intercollegiate athletics within the bounds of educational objectives.

"Athletic conferences were in constant search for the one formula that retained the advantages of athletics while eliminating the many faults inherent in its conduct."

Then, in 1932, the modern SEC was born, in Knoxville, Tennessee, on December 8 and 9. Ten schools east of the Appalachian Mountains became the Southern Conference, which would later split again and become the Atlantic Coast Conference. The other thirteen schools, those west of the mountains, became the Southeastern Conference. In February 1933, the Southern Conference treasurer transferred the funds of the thirteen SEC schools to the SEC treasurer, a princely sum of $2,077.78.

The SEC also devised its mission statement at a February 27, 1933, meeting at the Biltmore Hotel in Atlanta:

The Southeastern Conference is organized to form a more compact group of institutions with similar educational ideals in order that they may by joint action increase their ability to render the services for which they were founded and for which they are maintained, by making athletics a part of the educational plan and by making them subservient to the great aims and objects of education and placing them under the same administrative control.

Some rules were established. The season would not last longer than ten weeks. There was to be no scouting. Equipment could not be issued before the first Monday in September. Transfers were not permitted.

What happened next was monumental for college athletics, and the SEC got there first. The large southern schools decided to get payment of players out in the open and to award athletic scholarships, which would cover tuition, books, and room and board. A national uproar occurred, particularly from the schools of the Big Ten and in the West. Today the SEC is seen as too aggressive in college athletics, but in 1935 the SEC was regarded as pure evil for pushing forward the idea of paying players.

The same hypocrites from the Midwest and the East who poke at the SEC today existed eighty years ago.

"In the thirties when the SEC was giving scholarships, the Big

Ten and West Coast schools accused the southern schools of being openly professional. The southern schools accused them of being hypocritical because they were paying players by other means," said Mike Oriard, who played football at Notre Dame and is a retired English professor at Oregon State and has written several books on the culture of college football. "The Big Ten and West Coast schools weren't giving outright scholarships, but they were giving jobs sweeping the snow off the front walkway of the Coliseum in Los Angeles [where it doesn't snow]."

These no-show jobs were part of the culture of the Big Ten and eastern schools, yet southern schools were criticized when the SEC started to award scholarships in 1935.

"There were schools in this era who thought it was more ethical to have the athletes sponsored by alumni rather than being paid by institutional resources," Oriard said. "The Big Ten and the Pacific Coast schools had no problem with alumni providing jobs for young men. Somehow these young men would be tainted if they used institutional money."

Doyle said the South at the turn of the century and early in the twentieth century did not have the economic kingpins in communities who could pay players like the schools in the North. The universities finally had to pitch in if they wanted to grow their programs. Soon, the rest of college football followed the SEC and awarded athletic scholarships.

The SEC had a much more modest existence in the 1930s. Dues to join the SEC were $50. The one-day, one-night cost to attend the conference meeting was $9. It is a very different environment today. In May 2012, the SEC announced it was paying each of its members $20 million. Who needs dues?

The SEC in its first twenty years attempted to monitor and enforce eligibility rules and the illegal subsidizing of players, but on occasion misdeeds never got past the front gates of the university and ended up in the hands of the conference office. Take the issue of Bob Neyland, better known as General Robert Neyland, the legendary Tennessee football coach.

Ronald A. Smith, a professor emeritus of sports history at Penn State, told the *Washington Post* in November 2011 that he found in his search of University of Tennessee archives a "slush fund" Neyland used to pay players. When Tennessee president Cloide Brehm found out about the fund in the early 1950s, he called a meeting of his advisers. Smith said that in the transcript of the two-hour meeting, Brehm stated that Neyland "will resort to devious techniques to get what he wants and will give you the run-around and that makes it a difficult situation." Neyland retired as coach in 1952, but Brehm said evidence of the fund dated back to Neyland's first tenure as coach (1926 to 1934).

Brehm seemed terrified of his trustees and said that covering up for Neyland was essential. The trustees of the university would have "cut his throat" if news of the Neyland slush fund got out. Brehm was not about to let that happen. Many people feel the powerful football coach—the one who wins—has too much authority on campus today, but it was that way sixty, seventy, eighty years ago. It is not a new phenomenon.

The men who shaped the modern SEC were larger-than-life in eras gone by, and they are still with us. You see their names every day. Dudley is the name on the Vanderbilt football stadium. Sanford's name is on the University of Georgia stadium. Mike Donahue, the Auburn coach from 1904 to 1906 and 1908 to 1922, has a street named after him that cuts through campus. Neyland's name is on the Tennessee stadium.

Oriard said the conferences have gone from monitoring eligibility and settling disputes among rivals to becoming the driver of the economic engine. Oriard said the Pac-12 rather conspicuously turned away from maintaining academic standards to a stance of "We need to cash in on big bucks." It hired a businessman, Scott, to chase television deals and bring the money train into the Pac-12. The SEC was already at the station, of course.

Oriard said the university always had to backfill the Oregon State athletic department, but Scott's deals mean the Beavers can get $20 million a year from the Pac-12 as their share and depend less on university funds.

"The conferences, all of them, have gone from overseeing athletics, monitoring eligibility, to a position of maximizing revenues," Oriard said.

It seems only fitting that seventy-seven years later the SEC is making the most noise again for compensating the breadwinners of the athletic department. Steve Spurrier, the South Carolina coach, first proposed the idea of giving players a stipend in 2011. He brought it back to the other thirteen SEC coaches in May 2012 at the SEC's annual meeting, and the coaches voted unanimously, 14–0, to pay their players. Spurrier is proposing $3,000 to $4,000 for each player.

"We as coaches believe they're entitled to a little more than room, books, board, and tuition," Spurrier said. "Again, we as coaches would be willing to pay it if they were to approve it to where our guys could get approximately three thousand to four thousand bucks a year. It wouldn't be that much, but enough to allow them to live like normal student-athletes. We think they need more and deserve more. It's as simple as that."

The coaches, of course, do not want to make it possible for their athletes to have jobs, which is what "normal" students do when they need walk-around money, or money to go home for an emergency. Football is a full-time job at SEC schools, and in other conferences, and their training continues through the off-season (January to May) and picks up again in June and July. Some players do get part-time jobs, but their time is limited. The rest of college football is exploring the idea of paying players, but the sums the SEC is talking about dwarf what the rest of the country is considering.

That only figures. The South finished second once before. Ever since, it has been determined to finish first. Pride and football are not two separate things.

CHAPTER 2

GOLIATH'S BIG STEPS

Roy Kramer did not sleep well the last week in November 1992. How could he? It was partly his bright idea to widen the moat in front of undefeated Alabama and make the Tide play one more conference game that season. In other years, the 11-0 Crimson Tide would be joyriding toward the Sugar Bowl to play Miami for the national title. But now the top was not down for Bama, the sun was not out, and there was no joyride. The Tide were preparing for another SEC game and muttering all the way that somebody was out to get them.

Kramer, the SEC commissioner, with the backing of the university presidents in the SEC, had concocted this thing called the SEC Championship Game. Who had ever heard of such a thing in Division I? It looked reckless to make the SEC regular-season champion play another game, and Gene Stallings, the Alabama coach, did not let Kramer forget about it that week.

"Gene said, 'We're eleven and oh and we haven't won nothin','" Kramer said. "He was right. They had the best record in the conference, but they were not conference champions."

The day he found out the SEC was adding a twelfth game for

the winners of the two divisions, plus going to an eight-game conference schedule, Stallings emerged from the meeting where those details were finalized and declared in a somber tone, "The SEC will never win another national championship."

Majors had said the same thing in 1989, but for other reasons. The SEC was starting to stamp out more and more NFL-caliber players, particularly on defense. Crowds were revved up; stadiums shook and threatened visiting teams. It was hard to win . . . anywhere.

And now the caretakers of the SEC had created an obstruction for its champion. Ohio State, Michigan, Notre Dame, Miami, Florida State, and Southern Cal, the other powerhouses, could relax after eleven games. Alabama, and the SEC teams that would follow it to the gallows of this thing called the SEC Championship Game, had to reboot and win again in a conference postseason game proposed by Stallings's own conference. It meant Alabama, just a week after playing the hysteria-filled Iron Bowl with Auburn, would have to play again on Legion Field against Steve Spurrier and Florida.

In the same meeting from which Stallings emerged with much anguish, Spurrier looked across the table at Kramer and wondered if Kramer was violating some sort of NCAA law. "Is that legal?" the Ball Coach asked of the proposed championship game. When the other conferences found out about the SEC's plan for a title game, they discussed bringing a bylaw to the floor of the NCAA convention to stop it, which never happened. In today's climate, with the rest of college football fed up with the SEC's spending and winning six straight titles, the bylaw might have passed.

The game was legal. Kramer, who was the commissioner of the SEC from 1990 to 2002, saw championship games done in the lower divisions of college football, and he had looked up the NCAA bylaw allowing for a conference championship game and kept it in his back pocket. The SEC commissioner was skewered in some columns across the South for backing this extra game. The accusations flew. It was a money grab by the conference, and it would tie a ball and chain around the league's best team.

"It was a risk," Kramer said. He paused for a moment, then chuckled. "I told Antonio Langham he was my hero that week."

Langham was an Alabama defensive back. In the first SEC Championship Game on December 2, 1992, in a 21–21 game against Florida, Langham squatted on a pass route down the right hash marks. He was lying in the weeds waiting, and waiting, then jumped a pass by the Gators' Shane Matthews with 3:16 remaining in the fourth quarter. Langham snatched the pass for an interception and zigzagged his way down the Legion Field carpet for a 37-yard return for a touchdown. On this miserable night with chill and light rain, when Langham handed Alabama that 28–21 victory, Kramer slipped his head out of the noose and saw sunshine.

The Crimson Tide then went on to thump favored Miami, 34–13, to win the Sugar Bowl and claim the national championship with a 13-0 record.

Langham's interception was trumpeted as the play that saved the SEC's skin and promoted the glory of the championship game. There wasn't exactly a happy ending for the cornerback from Town Creek, Alabama, though. The next season, Langham helped Alabama to an 8-3-1 season with an all-American type year, but he got tangled up with an agent, which was against NCAA rules, and the NCAA came down on Alabama. Wins were forfeited amid sanctions and lost scholarships.

The Kramer Bowl, meanwhile, became a launching point for some SEC teams to win national championships. It was also a nationally televised game, which meant more exposure and, yes, more television money for the SEC. This big step for Goliath was another escalation of football on an academic campus, another week when students had to be athletes.

The SEC Championship Game was one last audition for voters before the final polls, and it came when many teams had finished their regular seasons. More than that, the SEC Championship Game and the eight-game schedule were booster rockets for the conference schools. Programs had to get better. They had to gear up more on Saturdays, and that meant recruiting harder and not making mistakes in recruiting. They had to raise the level of their game because of these extra conference games.

Look back at Bear Bryant's teams at Alabama. Those squads had to play just six conference games, then seven beginning in 1988 for four seasons. Sure, in some seasons Bryant scheduled Nebraska and Notre Dame, but for many years to win the SEC, the Crimson Tide, Tennessee, LSU, and all the rest had to play just six league games. Now, with eight games, it is really a gauntlet. By the time SEC teams get to the postseason, they have seen every gadget play, stonewall defenses, the best defensive linemen, hearty tailbacks, and keen-eyed coaches on the other sideline. These last six national champions, all SEC teams, have been worked over inside their own conference, and when they hit adversity in the title game, whether it was against Ohio State in January 2007 or Oregon in January 2011, they found a way to accelerate past trouble. The two extra games helped mobilize the SEC.

Just as important as adding a layer of steel with a longer SEC season, the SEC jumped out of its box as a regional football league. Until the Big 12, then the ACC and the Big Ten, and the Pac-12, added their own conference championship games, the SEC was on the national stage by itself with the SEC Championship Game in early December. When the game was moved to the Georgia Dome in 1994, it became a spectacle. Half the fans were in one school's colors, half were in another school's colors. The noise bounced off the marshmallow roof, down into the bowl, and the cheers were thunderous. National media attended the game and saw the spirit of the conference and took note.

· The Big Ten's reluctance to playing a conference championship game cost Michigan a chance to sway voters in 2006 when the one-loss Wolverines were passed over by Florida. There was an uproar in Ann Arbor, but there shouldn't have been. The Gators played a meaningful SEC Championship Game against Arkansas and its all-American running back Darren McFadden while Michigan sat at home that weekend. The Kramer Bowl put an SEC team in the line of fire for another week while the Wolverines had their feet up begging for a title shot. The Big Ten whined that Urban Meyer, the Florida coach, campaigned too much for his team to play Ohio State. The Florida players didn't think Meyer campaigned too much; he was working for them.

Michigan lost to Southern Cal, 32–18, in the Rose Bowl. Florida pounded Ohio State, 41–14, in the National Championship Game, the same Ohio State that beat Michigan, 42–39. It was another reason to again rejoice at the Kramer Bowl.

If Kramer thought Stallings and the other SEC coaches were mad at him, he soon had another crew ready to march on Birmingham. The other commissioners who made up the College Football Association got a jolt when the chairman of their television committee told them he was leaving their TV deal in 1995.

Kramer was that TV chairman and he was taking the SEC with him.

CBS, still stinging from losing its longtime NFL foothold, met with Kramer secretly in New York, and they worked out a deal. The SEC left the CFA for its own national deal, a landmark for the conference. It was money and exposure. The SEC was ringing up victories off the field, which was actually the cha-ching of the cash register.

"I had to call Chuck Neinas and tell him we signed with CBS," Kramer said. "He wasn't happy with me.

"Oh, we're still friends, but he was not happy." Neinas was the executive director of the CFA.

Then, the burgeoning cable network ESPN asked Kramer if the SEC would be willing to play some Saturday-night games. Why not? LSU loved to play at night. The Tigers think they invented night football. The staid, tradition-bound Big Ten played only day games on Saturday, but the SEC was more than willing to pay an extra electric bill for night football. The SEC was now on two national networks, another hallmark for the conference, another step forward for Goliath.

If it was all about TV money, Notre Dame would not be going on eighteen seasons without a national championship. The Irish signed their own TV deal with NBC. But the SEC's streak is more than TV money. In 2011, for the fourteenth straight year (among Football Bowl Subdivision teams), the SEC had the most fans with 6.3 million, or an average of 75,832 per game. The Big Ten was second (71,439), the Big 12 was third (63,265), the Pac-12 was fourth (52,249), and the ACC was fifth (51,406). That same year, CBS's national coverage of the SEC was the highest-rated regular-season college football package on any network for the third consecutive season.

Look some more at Kramer's creation. The SEC on CBS had the three highest-rated 2011 college football games: LSU vs. Alabama with an 11.5/20 rating/share; LSU vs. Georgia in the SEC Championship Game with a 7.3/15 rating/share; and LSU vs. Arkansas with a 6.3/15 rating/share.

When LSU played Alabama in the National Championship Game in January 2012, the event drew more than 24 million viewers and had the second-highest number of households viewing in cable television history, but it was also one of the lowest-rated National Championship Games in the fourteen-season era of the BCS. The rest of the country yawned at the rematch; the SEC reveled.

The SEC Championship Game created national exposure and swelled the conference bank account, but it also created late-season suspense inside the conference in the division races. More games mattered as teams made the hunt for Atlanta and the conference championship game a priority. If you won a division in the SEC, it meant you had successfully dealt with the likes of Alabama, Auburn, Florida, and Georgia and could play on the grand stage of the SEC Championship in Atlanta in early December. SEC schools are more than proud to hang "Eastern" or "Western" division championship banners, because it is not an easy thing to do in this conference.

Under Kramer's leadership, the SEC distributed $654 million in revenue to its members and won eighty-five national championships. Kramer is also regarded as one of the creators of the BCS, and that is something to be proud of, even with the uproar nationally for a postseason tournament in college football. The BCS had its faults, but at least it kept college football's regular season from being diluted into an NFL-style tournament. It maintained the intrigue of the regular season.

"We don't want to be college basketball," Kramer said. "Their season is down to one month, March, because of their tournament.

"Our entire regular season matters."

The SEC decided on something else in that 1990 meeting. It was not going to participate in every collegiate sport. Kramer and the athletic directors decided that the SEC was going to put its resources into certain sports and ambitiously hunt national championships. Men's soccer, for instance, was not a championship the SEC would pursue. The SEC doesn't just want to load up the trophy cabinet with football trophies; it wants to win in all the sports it participates in. Other conferences were carrying twenty-four or twenty-five sports, or more. SEC schools were sponsoring fewer sports, an average of twenty, which also meant they had more money for facilities and coaches' salaries for football.

Here is where the watchdogs of college athletics feel the SEC really got out of line with the rest of the country as it surged ahead in college football. It wasn't just the TV deals and coaches' contracts that rankled the caretakers of higher education. It was slicing away some other sports to put more money into revenue sports.

"The SEC has been the catalyst for an escalation of spending in a select number of sports that I think ultimately is going to break the current model of Division I athletics," said Amy Perko, executive director of the Knight Commission on Intercollegiate Athletics. She was referring to the broad-based programs that many departments support, gymnastics to softball to football. Perko made that comment in 2009. She stood by it June 2012.

The Knight Commission believes universities should follow the mandated philosophy of Division I and offer the broadest number of opportunities, perhaps more than the minimum required, which is sixteen sports.

Not only are the so-called nonrevenue sports losing some funding, but those sports are at the mercy of football for scheduling. It is one thing for the West Virginia football team to leave town on Friday for a game in Oklahoma, it is another thing for the Mountaineers' volleyball, tennis, baseball, and other sports teams to have to play in the Big 12 and balance schedules and academics. TV contracts for football are driving conference affiliation, but it is seriously impacting other sports on campus because they have to compete in those made-for-TV conferences.

Perko simply asks, "Is there a more appropriate model for the rest of the sports on campus?"

Mike Slive became SEC commissioner in 2002 and has shown some dexterity in dealing with the acrimony of SEC vs. Everyone Else. His first initiative was tackling the compliance issues that had been plaguing the conference. But while Slive was threatening schools by telling them he would aid the NCAA in investigations of their programs, he was building the brand even stronger by making the SEC more relevant to its fans with celebrations off the field. The SEC pushed forward the colors and traditions of schools. At the same time, it paid attention to minority hiring. Soon, it wasn't just football gaining momentum, it was the whole conference, and sponsors rushed in to be part of the gusher of fan enthusiasm for the SEC. The SEC became richer and richer with Slive holding the rudder.

"We are now walking down Main Street, not a back alley," Slive said.

While other conferences kept sniping at the SEC, Slive kept pushing forward initiatives that benefited athletes as he tried to balance out the overindulgence of SEC football with the academic mission. The recent rallying cry among the BCS conferences for multiyear scholarships last fall in an NCAA presidential retreat came *after* Slive's address to the media in July 2011 that said schools should explore multiyear scholarships. Of course, it was the Knight Commission that first pushed for five-year scholarships way back in 1991.

In addition to the multiyear-scholarship proposal, the SEC wanted to study whether players who are admitted to schools and at risk academically should be made to sit their freshman season while they got some traction in classes and learned how to apply themselves. The Knight Commission got there first, too, twenty years ago, but at least the issue is resurfacing and the wealthy SEC is not standing in the way.

Slive also proposed a "full analysis of a prospect's academic performance throughout his or her high school career to give us a better picture and more complete picture of the individual's preparation for college work."

In its October 2011 meeting, the NCAA board agreed to make high school seniors have a 2.3 GPA and have completed ten of sixteen core courses before their senior season. That was an SEC proposal. If these entrance guidelines had been in place, 40 percent of Division I freshmen would have been academic redshirts. That news did not get much attention, but it should have. High school players now have until 2016 to wise up, or they will sit a year and lose a season of eligibility.

I am not always a big fan of the SEC because football coaches wring everything they can out of players during the week and make it extremely difficult for them to put in a well-rested effort in the classroom, but you have to give some credit to the SEC for some athlete-welfare reforms. The SEC wants to allow athletic departments to provide aid to former players for however long it takes that athlete to complete the requirements for a degree. The NCAA rule is that aid can be provided no longer than six years after initial enrollment. The SEC wants that limit ended, which is vital for the player who leaves school after his junior year for the NFL and wants to come back to finish school. How many times have you read about the former NFL player who has squandered his money four, five, six years after he has stopped playing? Some of it has to do with taking care of family, or a lack of self-control with sudden riches.

Most of it is a lack of a backup plan that a finished education can provide.

The SEC coaches voted on May 31, 2012, to pay players some of the millions of dollars raked in by football. Perhaps their guilt was finally too much to bear. They didn't want to give the players the summer off to work jobs like other students to earn spending money; they want them on campus lifting weights and throwing footballs. Coaches insist one of the reasons players need to be on campus in the summer is to take an extra class or two. That would not be necessary if football were not a full-time job in the fall and the players could bear down on academics. It's true, the majority of players want to be on campus building their bodies, but some of that has to do with staying competitive with the guy above or below them on the depth chart. Scholarships are year to year, after all, and players can be cut loose from their scholarship. It's all a web, you see.

More recently, the SEC has dealt with the issue of oversigning of high school prospects by the conference's coaches. Recruits at some schools were suddenly being told there was no room for them and they had to "grayshirt," or wait until January to get scholarship money. The coaches wanted to make sure they had their full complement of scholarship players by the time August practice started. If four players flunked out at the end of the school year, well, that was okay because the recruiting class had twenty-nine, or four extra bodies. The coaches have a valid point that some players needed to be kicked out of the program for discipline issues at the end of the school year, which made some wiggle room necessary. In those spring months when guardrails are down, football players can get in trouble or fail classes and need to be excused from the program. Still, even with some dismissals, that might leave approximately eighty scholarship players, and that sure seems like enough to field a football team. The NFL makes it work with far fewer players on the roster.

The conference office and most athletic directors, who saw the integrity of the conference attacked nationally, put the coaches in their place with a stiffer oversigning rule. Watchdog websites such as Oversigning.com created a PR wart for SEC schools that oversigned. The SEC forwarded legislation to the NCAA to make oversigning a national issue, which was only fitting because SEC coaches had been accused the most often of crushing dreams on signing day, even though other BCS conferences had plenty of offenders.

The oversigning legislation was approved in January 2012 by the NCAA Legislative Council and Board of Directors and will be in effect nationally for signing day in 2013.

SEC schools also get hammered for pushing players off the scholarship roll for bogus medical reasons. Greg Sankey, the associate commissioner and the SEC's operations director, has maintained that SEC programs are not being allowed to willy-nilly discard players under the guise of false medical conditions. Sankey said all SEC schools have to petition the conference office when they want a player taken off their scholarship count for medical reasons. The conference office has its own doctors and medical professionals review the petitions.

"We *have* turned down schools who have petitioned for a medical redshirt and we *will* do it again," Sankey said.

Charles Davis, a former player at Tennessee and now an analyst for college football and the NFL, said the SEC has thrived because Slive has stood up to the SEC coaches on issues of oversigning and has stood up to commissioners from the other conferences who want to damage the SEC's reputation.

Slive has fought at every turn the perception the SEC is a band of cheaters, but what the SEC and the NCAA allowed to happen with the Cam Newton situation in November 2010 was indefensible. That was a step back for Goliath, a giant step back, because the integrity of the conference office was called into question after seven years of hard work to clean up its reputation.

First, the SEC let the Newton saga boil over. Mississippi State said it told the SEC in January 2010 that Newton's father, Cecil, was shopping his son as a quarterback and wanted to be paid. The SEC said it was waiting for more information from Mississippi State before it could act and was following protocol, so it allowed Newton to start the 2010 season. Why? There was a hint of a violation. More than a few people felt the SEC should have acted faster. Slive hesitated to act because Mississippi State broke protocol by notifying the NCAA first of a possible violation before the SEC. Slive thought because the issue was already in the hands of the NCAA he didn't need to push Mississippi State, but there could have been a resolution long before November 2010 when Auburn was in the thick of the national championship race and the Newton controversy ruled the headlines. It led to the perception that the SEC took its time so Newton could play. As it was, he won the Heisman Trophy and had one of the greatest seasons in the history of college football, perhaps the greatest season ever for a player.

Still, not even a major scandal could tip the SEC off its secure pedestal atop college football. Slive and the presidents have maximized revenues and enhanced the SEC brand with sponsors. The money flow is an open spigot. In 2008, the SEC announced fifteen-year television deals with CBS and ESPN worth at least $3 billion. The other conferences have caught up or are catching up with the SEC in revenue, and it remains to be seen what the Pac-12, for instance, does with the windfall from its TV deals. Will it direct schools to put funds back into football and push back on the SEC?

Look at Arizona, a Pac-12 school. The Wildcats, according to December 2011 data compiled by *USA Today*, paid their football staff $2.9 million. Alabama paid its staff $8.5 million. Look at a smaller-revenue SEC school, such as Arkansas. The Razorbacks still paid their staff $3 million more than Arizona State, another Pac-12 school. The Pac-12 has a TV deal worth $250 million a year. Are the schools going to use that money to close the gap with the SEC, expand stadiums, increase the recruiting budget, and pay coaches more money?

Time will tell. There is still a culture difference. Football in the South eats and eats and eats. SEC football has too big of a head start on the Pac-12 for money to make a difference.

Southern Cal will win a national championship, or maybe Oregon, and the Pac-12 will claim it is in the same league with the SEC, but it won't be true. The SEC took all the important steps first, which included conference presidents' making the decision to pay coaches more money.

"The presidents allowed football to be the front porch for the schools," Davis said.

In December 2011, the SEC coaches had seats in plush leather on the front porch and half the conference coaches had salaries of more than $3 million, which included the disgraced and fired Arkansas coach Bobby Petrino. For several years, Iowa's Kirk Ferentz was the only Big Ten coach with a salary over $3 million, but he has recently been joined by Michigan's Brady Hoke ($3.2 million average over six years) and Ohio State's Urban Meyer, the first $4 million coach in the Big Ten. The football fiefdoms in the SEC, operating under their own tent on campus, raise the money and give some back to the school's general fund, but they keep most of it.

Two other landmark events occurred for the SEC besides the hiring of Roy Kramer, the SEC Championship Game, the ESPN/CBS deals, and the hiring of Mike Slive.

LSU's hiring of Nick Saban, which brought one of the country's best coaches into the SEC, was a huge step. He has won national championships at two SEC schools and, just as important, brought an NFL mind-set into building a roster through height, weight, speed, and strength and conditioning and hard coaching. The hallmarks of Saban's teams have been big, fast backs (Mark Ingram, Trent Richardson) and just plain large people who could move their feet (Marcell Dareus, Terrence Cody, Rolando McClain, Dont'a Hightower, Courtney Upshaw, among others). The rest of the SEC has had to get better to keep up with Saban, who will be remembered as one of the greatest coaches in the history of the game. He is winning national championships when the competition for titles is fierce.

Florida's hiring of Urban Meyer during a time when Meyer, a Midwest-bred coach, was expected to go to Notre Dame was a coup for the SEC. The Gators' checkbook and fertile recruiting ground—plus having the best athletic director in the SEC—trumped whatever the Irish could offer in terms of tradition. It helped that his family preferred Florida over South Bend, Meyer said.

It was the second time Florida athletic director Jeremy Foley had stepped up and secured a coach for the Gators. In 1997, with the NFL buzzing around Spurrier, Foley paid Spurrier $1.94 million a season. At the time, only the New York Jets' Bill Parcells ($3.3 million) and the Miami Dolphins' Jimmy Johnson ($2 million) made more money as football coaches. Spurrier had already turned down the Saints, and he stayed in Gainesville until he resigned in January 2002. Ten days later,

Spurrier signed the richest coach's contract in the history of the NFL (five years, $25 million), with the Washington Redskins.

The SEC's march to the top of college football was because of everything from television contracts to coaches' contracts to aggressive recruiting to a conference championship game, and it started with Kramer and the Kramer Bowl. Others have come along after Kramer and kept the fuel in the tank for the SEC, but Kramer was the first to walk out on the ledge—with the push from the presidents of the SEC. He was in charge when the conference split into divisions, created a championship game, and went to the eight-game schedule. It all helped grow the conference into Goliath, and now the rest of the country is trying to catch up with expansion and their own aggressive TV deals. They all—the Pac-12, Big 12, Big Ten—feel content they have caught or passed the SEC in TV profits, but the SEC hasn't even cashed that chip called the SEC Network, which is on the way, and then the rest of college football will have to catch up again.

Kramer pushed away his lunch plate and leaned forward when asked to explain the significance of the first SEC Championship Game and the revolution that was started.

"It elevated people's awareness of our league," he said. "That first championship game, the SEC was on a national stage with nothing to compete against us. The commissioner of the NFL was there at the first game. Keith Jackson called the game on TV. Football in the South was big long before I was around, but this game elevated our conference some more.

"There's a pride when you hear, 'SEC, SEC, SEC.' You don't just hear it at football games, you hear it at the Final Four, you hear it in Omaha at the College World Series when we play there. You feel good about that."

CHAPTER 3

GROWING THE SEC

Once upon a time, the Major League Baseball scouts could drive through the American South and have a decent chance of finding the five-tool player, the high school junior or senior who could run, hit for average, hit for power, throw, and wield the glove. These were the 6-foot-1, 6-foot-2, 200-to-220-pound athletes who could bat third in the lineup and play third base, right field, or center field and carry a team. Some of these high school ballplayers could walk away from a nice signing bonus in baseball to play college football, but it was not an easy thing to do. Bo Jackson, an African American athlete, walked away from baseball's big money once, but that was because Auburn coach Pat Dye told his seniors to take the freshman into the mountains for some fishing the weekend the Yankees wheeled their money into town to try to sign him. It was also because Bo's mom told him he was going to college.

Many other kids stuck with baseball back in the day, the sixties, seventies, and early eighties, and took the bonus money and endured the bus rides in the bush leagues. Sometimes they made it to the bigs. Most of the time they didn't.

Then the Southeastern Conference started to build itself into a nifty brand with new coats of paint for monolithic football stadiums and polished weight rooms and fewer restraints on the number of black athletes on its rosters. High school football coaches paid attention and became enablers for the SEC programs. In the seventies and early eighties, the SEC schools started to hand out more of their precious scholarships to black athletes, and high school football coaches talked their players off the diamond and onto the gridiron. As more scholarships went out to the black athlete—and a chance at an education—the number of blacks in baseball started to decline. If you graphed it, you could see the hijackings of baseball talent right there on a sheet of paper. The line goes down, down, down, from 1979 to the present day.

In 1979, Major League Baseball rosters included approximately 28 percent African Americans. In 1990, it was 17 percent. In 2011, it was 8.5 percent. In 2012, the number of African Americans dropped to 8 percent, the lowest figure since shortly after the integration of the game by Jackie Robinson in 1947.

In an interview in 2006, Clarence Johns, a national scout for the Texas Rangers, said twenty years ago he could drive through the South and find plenty of black athletes still playing baseball. Six years ago, at the start of this SEC streak of national championships in football, Johns was attending a black baseball showcase in Atlanta and talked about the lamentable change in color in the game. Steve Williams, who was a scout for the Kansas City Royals at the time, nodded in agreement during the discussion. He was president of the Buck O'Neil Professional Scouts and Coaches Association, named for the legendary Negro League player Buck O'Neil, and Williams said he understood the impact of football, too. Many wanted to blame racism for the declining number of black players in baseball, but Williams would not easily jump to that conclusion.

"Nineteen years ago when I started scouting in South Carolina, I could find baseball players, but when the college football programs started putting more money into their programs, the high school coaches started pushing their kids into football," said Williams, who is now with the Pittsburgh Pirates. "They pushed and they pushed and they got them into spring football and into track. They didn't want them in baseball."

There are exceptions. James Phillips, the father of the Cincinnati Reds' second baseman Brandon Phillips, had to chase away the football coaches as they tried to recruit his son, a middle school star as a running back. The coaches sent Brandon home with football pads, and Phillips made his son take them back the next day. Brandon Phillips stuck with baseball and signed a $72 million contract with the Reds in April 2012.

Look at Mobile, Alabama. It was a nurturing ground for baseball. Hank Aaron, baseball's legitimate home-run champion, was the city's biggest hero, but Satchel Paige came out of the Mobile area, as did other black players, such as Billy Williams, Tommie Agee, Amos Otis, Ozzie Smith, and Willie McCovey. The playgrounds were teeming with baseball talent, until football started to take over in the eighties and nineties.

"Mobile is no longer a baseball town," said Phil Savage, a Mobile native and the executive director of the Senior Bowl, which is played in Mobile, former general manager of the Cleveland Browns, and college scout and assistant coach. "It is a football town now."

Where did the rest of the baseball talent go? College basketball programs, big and small, took some athletes. Then there are the fledgling football programs in the South that have joined Division I since 2005: Georgia State, Kennesaw State (GA), Florida International, Florida Atlantic, South Alabama, University of Texas/ San Antonio, and Western Kentucky. Troy University, which is near Montgomery, Alabama, joined Division I in 2002 and is a haven for many southern-bred high school players.

But the biggest benefactor in the decline of baseball in the South among athletes of all colors was SEC football. As a freshman on a college baseball team, they could sweep up the sunflower seeds in the dugout after a chilly February game; or as football players, they could rush out to the field through a tunnel to ninety thousand adoring fans who would wrap their arms around them.

Chris Smelley, of course, picked the fans and the adoration. He was a star catcher in high school in Alabama, but also a star quarterback. Smelley had a chance to play quarterback for Steve Spurrier at South Carolina. When Mike Shula, the former Alabama coach, kept chasing Tim Tebow as his quarterback of the future, Smelley signed with Spurrier.

"We wanted him, but it's hard to give up being a quarterback at a big school in the South. We've had to deal with this before," said Jim Wells, the former Alabama baseball coach, who retired in 2009.

"Even Mickey Mantle had to think about what he was going to do," said Wells, referring to the Yankee star from Commerce, Oklahoma, who was offered scholarships to play college football. "It is a hard thing to lay down, even if your future is in the other sport."

Smelley was back in Alabama after several fitful seasons of trying to satisfy the taskmaster Spurrier. He joined the Alabama baseball team and picked up the sport again from scratch as a backup catcher.

"There's a big difference playing in front of ninety thousand and playing in front of a few thousand," Smelley said. "That will be one of the things I miss."

The SEC did not just take from baseball, it took from above the Mason-Dixon Line, too, the states hit by economic downturn and instability in the last ten years.

On the website of the Population Reference Bureau (www.prb .org), the US census of 2010 shows South Carolina with a population jump of 15.3 percent in the last decade, Georgia with an 18.3 percent increase, and Florida with a bump of 17.6 percent. Compare that to Michigan, which lost 0.6 percent of its population from 2000 to 2010, and Ohio, which gained just 1.6, and Pennsylvania, which gained a mere 3.4 percent.

Think about the shutting of steel mills and what that meant to the local high schools in Pennsylvania. Western Pennsylvania was the breeding ground for sensational quarterbacks such as Joe Namath, Johnny Unitas, Joe Montana, and Dan Marino, and many other players who were not quarterbacks. Have you heard much from that area of the country with the decline in population? Alabama thumped Penn State in 2010 and 2011, and the Nittany Lions and Pittsburgh, national contenders back in the eighties and nineties, have fallen off the chase for the national championship.

Look at the most recent state added to the SEC footprint: Texas. It saw a jump in population from 2000 to 2010 of 20.6 percent. Texas A&M joined the SEC in 2012, which means the SEC has access to even more players.

South Carolina is a right-to-work state, antiunion, and new companies flocked there to avoid clashes with unions in the North and to pay less. Employers in South Carolina have more favorable laws. Companies such as BMW moved in and planted roots, causing the population of the state to swell, which meant a few more defensive tackles growing up in the SEC heartland.

Gil Brandt, the former Dallas Cowboys executive (1960–1989) and NFL.com analyst, said that when he visits Canton, Ohio, he can just tell there is dwindling population by the lack of activity on the streets. Brandt says a stark difference exists between Canton and Dallas, specifically in a place called Frisco, Texas. Where there were tumbleweeds twenty-five years ago, there are now six high schools, he said. Football is thriving with the addition of more rooftops.

The population increase in the South was 14.3 percent compared to 3.9 in the Midwest and 3.2 in the Northeast from 2000 to 2010. Naturally, the South had a better chance to harvest tailbacks and defensive linemen because there were more people.

When I started this book, I thought the talent pool was deep all across the South and the population quake in the South was a significant reason the SEC was dominating college football. But it is not just numbers.

Dr. Mark Mather of the PRB said the fastest growth in the last two decades has occurred in the Southwest and the Mountain West, so the idea the SEC programs are clubbing programs from other conferences because they have a deeper talent pool might not exactly be true. If all it took was people power, Brigham Young, among others, would have a national champion (Utah came close with two undefeated teams).

In another statistic sent by the PRB, 18 percent of public elementary and secondary school students were in the nine-state SEC footprint (which does not include recently added Texas and Missouri). So, the high schools within the SEC boundaries are not overwhelming California, Texas, or Arizona with sheer numbers of players to choose from.

Some high schools in the South have increasing enrollments, especially in the Atlanta and Orlando areas, but the overwhelming of Ohio State, the University of Oklahoma, and the University of Oregon on the football field with numbers of high school players is *not* the only fuel for Goliath. Indeed, a four-thousand-student high school offers plenty of students to choose from, but if there is no culture, no drive for football, what good are the numbers? There has to be other fuel.

The other fuel is the passion of fans and the passion of coaches, whether it is on the youth, high school, or college level. The ferociousness with which they approach the game in the South—on the field and off the field—separates this section of the country from the rest. The Big Ten found that out all winter long in 2011–12 as the former Florida coach Urban Meyer hunted recruits for Ohio State, even when those high school players had committed to other Big Ten schools. Big Ten coaches were bitter at the "SEC way" of doing things. This hard-fought turf war was something a few schools in the Big Ten were apparently not accustomed to.

One scene illustrates how aggressive the SEC could be in recruiting, and it started well before this run of six championships. Peyton Manning had just made his official visit to Tennessee. The next morning Archie Manning, Peyton's father, was having breakfast with the Tennessee head coach, Phillip Fulmer, and offensive coordinator David Cutcliffe, the coach who groomed Peyton for the NFL, when one of the coach's aides stopped by the table and said an ice storm would prevent Fulmer from flying North to visit a recruit.

Fulmer was livid. After breakfast, he poked a finger at David Blackburn, who was in UT football operations, and said, "You better find me somebody to recruit today if I can't make this trip. You find them right now."

Fulmer did not want to waste one day during recruiting season. "I think those guys work on three or four hours' sleep a night during that recruiting period," Archie Manning said. "Phillip was a relentless recruiter. He had his mind on recruiting every day. They're all like that. Saban is like that. Les Miles is like that."

That is the kind of fuel that powers the SEC.

Here is some more fuel. The SEC has led Division I football in attendance for fourteen straight seasons. It averaged 75,832 fans per game, followed by the Big Ten (71,439), the Big 12 (63,265), Pac-12 (52,249), and ACC (51,406). The SEC fans do not just follow their team at home. When they travel, they cram into seats in the corners of the end zones every Saturday. SEC fans can jump in their cars and travel for just about any game. You couldn't do that in the Big Ten (Nebraska to Penn State), or ACC (Boston College to Miami), or Pac-10 (Oregon to Arizona). We'll see how rabid SEC fans are when they load up the car for the trip from South Carolina to Texas A&M, or Missouri. We'll see if for once Goliath bit off more than it can chew.

The rabid fan base, which buys tickets and adds eyeballs to TV games (and attracts sponsors), means the SEC has more $3-million-a-year salaried coaches (five) than any other conference.

The fan base means the SEC has a combined TV contract with CBS and ESPN for $3 billion over fifteen years. That contract is going to be renegotiated now with Texas A&M and Missouri joining the conference. There will be even more money later if the SEC, as expected, puts together its own TV network.

The fans' fuel runs athletic departments at SEC schools with revenues ranging from Mississippi State's $58 million to Alabama's approximately $124 million. Georgia has a $92 million budget, but charges students just $2 for basketball games and $8 for football and gives $5 million to $6 million back to the general fund of the university every year.

Now look at Clemson, which has a large stadium, but plays in the ACC, which is still a basketball league. The Tigers' athletic department revenue is around $61 million. Compare that to the median athletic department budget in the SEC, which is approximately $90 million, from 2009–10 data.

Five SEC schools have revenues over $100 million, while Arkansas and Georgia are around $92 million, according to *USA Today* (Vanderbilt is a private school and does not report). Football is the backbone of those budgets, and it pays for the so-called country-club sports on campus. The debate then starts about how African American football players are paying for the scholarships in other sports for the white athletes from upper-income backgrounds. You could write another book about that.

How else has the SEC grown? Does it benefit from better weather? You can't deny that. The South has more days during the school year for high school players to get outside for fall and spring practice. In Georgia it means ten extra practice days for high school teams, but then you have to count the days players are on a field themselves playing 7-on-7, or just working out inside the weight room with coaches.

That's fuel.

But what's done with that weather and money is more important. It goes into player development, and where there are NFL-caliber players, there are winning college programs.

Brandt ran the draft numbers from 2002 to 2011. Thirty-one schools produced 52 percent of the NFL draft picks. Southern California led with 69, followed by Ohio State with 66, and Miami with 63. Georgia was fourth with 57 and LSU was fifth with 56.

Four schools from the SEC, and three schools from the ACC, were in the top ten schools for draft picks in the ten-year cycle.

But Brandt also did a value index, which rated the quality of the drafts for each school, or how high those picks went. The difference between conferences was more stark. Five of the top eleven schools in the value index were from the SEC. The ACC and the Big 12 each had two schools in the top eleven of Brandt's index.

Southern California was first in the value index with 212 points in drafts from 2002 to 2011. Miami was second with 204 points, and Ohio State was third at 178, which is one from each conference. Then came Florida, LSU, and Georgia—three from the SEC—compared to one each from the Pac-12, the ACC, and the Big Ten.

Alabama was eleventh on the Brandt value index, but the Tide is rising in all draft equations the longer Nick Saban coaches in Tuscaloosa. Chris Samuels, an offensive lineman, and Shaun Alexander, a running back, were drafted in the first round in 2000, and the Tide did not have another first-round pick until offensive tackle Andre Smith in 2009, which followed Saban's second season. Alabama has had eleven first-round picks from 2009 to 2012 under Saban. Soon, Alabama could be at the top of Brandt's value index.

———

Brandt also looked at the population of different states and the number of NFL players from each state. The SEC was dominant again. Louisiana had the most players in the NFL, per capita. Mississippi was second, Florida was fourth, South Carolina was fifth, Alabama was sixth, and Georgia was seventh.

"If you do it by population, then Florida, Texas, and California are going to have the most NFL guys just by the sheer numbers," Brandt said. "You do it per capita and you get a look at states that can produce players without the huge population numbers. And you can see in that list where a lot of players come from, right there in SEC territory."

What is important, too, is the number of SEC schools sending players to the NFL. It is not just the powerhouses such as Alabama, LSU, Georgia, and Florida. The pros can come from Vanderbilt, Ole Miss, Mississippi State, and Kentucky. The SEC was the only BCS conference to have a player drafted from every team in 2012. Former LSU and NFL receiver Michael Clayton said he understands why.

"There are guys who wanted to go to LSU and to Alabama and Florida who maybe didn't get recruited by those schools," Clayton said. "There were only a certain amount of scholarships at those schools, so there was no room. They still wanted to play in the SEC and play against the best so they would get better and prepare for the NFL, so what they do is sign with another SEC school, maybe Mississippi or Mississippi State.

"So, you see, the SEC was getting the best players and it was getting the second-best players. We talked about it all the time in the NFL. You get a lot of athletic football players from the South. A lot of dominant players are found here, and not just at the schools like LSU and Alabama."

Darius Philon, a defensive lineman from Mobile, had expected to sign with Alabama in February 2012. When the Crimson Tide signed a defensive lineman from Virginia it rated higher, it did not offer Philon a scholarship for the start of the 2012–13 season, but asked him to delay and enter school the following January. Philon chose to take an offer from Arkansas instead. That was one side of the story. The other side of the story is that Alabama said it asked Philon to wait to sign because he had to undergo knee surgery and needed time to rehabilitate. Justin Taylor, a high school running back from Atlanta, expected to sign with Alabama, too. But when the Tide pulled his offer after an injury and asked him to delay his signing, Taylor signed with Kentucky, another SEC school. Either way, both players ended up in the talent-rich SEC.

Clayton, who lives in Tampa, said twenty years ago the SEC schools were also getting the first generation of black athletes who had a chance to get a college degree, the first in their family to go to school in some cases. In this epic occurrence, not only could they get on campus, but they could stay close to home, where their families could watch them play.

"For the past twenty years, you hear more and more in our churches that you have to get an education or you're going to be a repeat of your mother and your father," Clayton said. "Take that scholarship, get an education, break the curse, break the cycle. It weighs heavily on kids. It is no surprise that black kids are going to get that education and use football to do it."

The constant argument is that football is a plantation sport with black players enriching white coaches, white sponsors, and white businesses, not to mention the white athletes in the country-club sports on campus (the golf team does not pay its way). That point of view has some validity when football players are herded into academic majors to keep them eligible, not to educate them and push them toward a legitimate degree.

In 2006, the *New York Times* looked at the free and easy courses offered to football players at Auburn, and coach Tommy Tuberville insisted it was a nonstory. Still, Auburn was forced to investigate the issue of easy-A courses. Not just black students were being handed an easy grade, but white players, too. Auburn claimed many students on campus took self-directed courses, not just athletes, but that the football players clustered around one teacher was suspicious.

The steering of football players to easy classes in the summer to lessen their academic load in the fall and keep them eligible is one of the worst offenses and a truly shameful aspect of college football. In 2008, *USA Today* did a landmark study of athletes—not just in football—who were clustered into easy majors and shepherded through college, and the resentment the athletes felt when their eligibility was up. They felt cheated because the athlete-only degrees—social science majors more often than not—did not prepare athletes for life after college. It was a rip-off, but it occurred across the college athletics landscape, not just in the SEC.

Clayton, who is writing a book on his experiences in life and athletics in college and the NFL, said black athletes flocked toward athletics in elementary and high school because it was fun, but also because it got them on equal footing with whites in at least one arena in life.

"If you were an African American with ability, it gave people of the other race a reason to look beyond your color and consider you an equal," Clayton said. "That's not to say that is a good thing, but it was a privilege in the black community to be looked at as an equal. It was a great feeling to be taken care of and treated like you were wanted and belonged somewhere and that you were needed.

"If you were a normal black kid, you were judged in communities. You were racially profiled. To the African American community, being accepted was motivation to try harder. Being an athlete gave you a chance to be the first in your family to get an education and then to take care of your family. Those football scholarships opened a lot of doors."

Added Clayton, "We're proud to be black, but it's not easy."

Black players are certainly not the only ones attracted to football and the SEC. Far from it.

White players also enjoy the game and make sacrifices in high school to train so they can get a college scholarship. No matter what your color, playing college football, especially in the SEC, is prestigious in the South.

But while black players play for their community, white players might play for the South and the pride of being from Tennessee, Alabama, Mississippi, or Florida. There is a distinct difference.

"I think the white players are more wrapped up in the mythological aspect of football than the black kids," said Allen Tullos, a professor of American studies at Emory University, who has an undergraduate degree from Alabama and an advanced degree from Yale. "For the black kids it can be a sport, but also a way out. For the white kids, it is a sport but also an 'us against them' thing, part of the southern male identity. Us against the North. In this part of the country where education is undervalued and undersupported, boys' success in sports, particularly football, brings recognition.

"It is also a test of manhood. 'Go and be the toughest, and after you've been through this, you are going to be a leader for life.' "

That football is intertwined with manliness, Tullos said, is a pervasive thought in the South he grew up in. "There is an emphasis on hard physical work and on hard 'play' that can quickly turn violent. Football goes with the manly culture, the hunting culture, the military culture. There is the animosity to gun control, too, and the practice of not calling the law to handle things, but to handle it yourself."

Former SEC commissioner Roy Kramer said one of his close

friends, the late *Knoxville News-Sentinel* columnist Tom Siler, often wrote about the passion of football fans in the South.

"Football was part of the recovery of pride in the South one hundred years ago, ninety years, eighty years ago," Kramer said. "They were building a cultural pride, and if you were from Alabama, you said, 'That's my state, that's my team.' There is something to that, I think."

In 1910, Vanderbilt was playing Yale in New Haven, Connecticut, a game that ended in a scoreless tie. In his book *Southeastern Conference Football: America's Most Competitive Conference*, John D. McCallum writes that a few minutes before kickoff, the Vandy coach Dan McGugin told his players that some of their grandfathers were sleeping (dead) in the military cemeteries of the North.

McGugin pointed across the field at the Yale players and said, "And there are the grandsons of the damn Yankees who put them there."

Gil Brandt, who lives in the Dallas area, scouted the South and came to understand the mythological impact of football. The roots were deep, planted by the legendary coaches, Tennessee's General Neyland and Alabama's Bear Bryant and the Ole Miss coach John Vaught, among others, but also by many other proud men and women of the South. There was no NFL south of Washington, DC, to interfere with the planting of those roots in the twenties, thirties, forties, and fifties.

"The history carries over, from grandfather, to father, to son," Brandt said. "It is still totally amazing to me the emphasis on football within families. I have never seen it like it is in the South, so widespread. I think you have some great traditions in Ohio, but the Midwest states are descending states in average age, and it seems there are more young families in the South carrying on that tradition."

What cannot be denied is that both black and white players have contributed to the success of the Southeastern Conference. And both black and white players did not just show up on SEC campuses, right out of the womb, able to play football. They were taught football from an early age, and they were taught in junior high and high school about the sacrifices needed to be a good player. No one had to say the summer weight-lifting workouts were mandatory because the kids found their way to the weight rooms on their own, eager to get stronger and faster so they could make the team. Nothing came with a guarantee of a college scholarship, but they gave themselves a chance to succeed, if not in Division I football, then with a school in the Football Championship Series (formerly I-AA), or Division II, or Division III, or NAIA, or junior college.

"When I was at Alabama as a graduate assistant coach years ago, there was such a respect factor among the players and the coaches," said Phil Savage, the executive director of the Senior Bowl, former general manager of the Cleveland Browns, and college scout and assistant coach. "College football was the only game in town, and it means something to the players. Football is a huge focus.

"When I went to UCLA as an assistant, the kids had the same respect, 'Yes, sir' and 'No, sir,' and they loved the game, but when there were seven pro teams in L.A. and Orange County, UCLA football was just something that was a pastime. People can do a lot of things; there is not quite the cultural emphasis on football out West as there is in the South. That cultural difference means something. There are great coaches across the country, but in a general, very general way, I think players are coached harder in the Southeast. There are some hard-knock high school coaches here, and the players are weathered a little bit."

The players get to college with some seasoning and training

from knowledgeable youth league coaches, middle school coaches, and high school coaches. The high school football programs in the South have been training their up-and-coming players since they were six or seven years old, at least at the powerhouse high schools spread around the South: Grayson High School in Loganville, Georgia; Armwood in Seffner, Florida; Plant in Tampa, Florida; Trinity in Louisville; Carroll in Southlake, Texas; Stephenson in the Atlanta area; Miami Central; Byrnes in Duncan, South Carolina; Valdosta and Lowndes in south Georgia; Spain Park in the Birmingham, Alabama, area; Daphne in the Mobile, Alabama, area; and Prattville, Alabama. High school football coaches at some programs in the South are routinely paid $100,000 a year or more.

Grayson, which is thirty miles east of Atlanta, was built in 2000 and won its first Class 5A state championship in 2011 after several near misses. The head coach is Mickey Conn, originally from Gadsden, Alabama, who played high school football in Gwinnett County, Georgia. His program is at a level where eleven thousand fans came out for a regular-season game against Brookwood High School in 2011.

Coincidentally or not, Conn played football in the SEC at Alabama. He played in the first SEC Championship Game in 1992, when Alabama beat Florida at Legion Field in Birmingham, 28–21. Conn made the first tackle ever in the SEC Championship Game, which was on kickoff coverage.

Here is what's vital to the successful southern program: Conn does not size players up when they get to him in the ninth grade. He has an understanding of players well before. He has followed them since they were six years old. He understands their makeup mentally as players as much as he understands their physical tools. Conn knows who works hard and shows resiliency under pressure.

"Our varsity coaches are staying after the high school practice to work with youth league players as young as six years old, and some of the coaches have kids who play," Conn said. "They teach them our offense and teach them the drills we do.

"We are teaching the fundamentals of blocking and tackling at six. They are taught to drive block and how to get off the ball and get their hands on the defensive lineman. They are taught how to keep a wide base with board drills and how to tackle; hit them high where they live."

When Conn and his coaches put the names of players in the Grayson program up on a depth-chart board in May 2012, the number of players in all grade levels was staggering: 230. The Rams dressed 110 for home games in 2011 and took 80 to away games.

A board of directors helps choose the coaches for Grayson's six-, seven-, and eight-year-olds. Dads do not just jump out of the stands and run drills. Conn opens up the facility to the youth teams to use blocking sleds and tackling dummies. The weight training starts in the seventh grade.

"We don't know how good they are going to be when they are six or seven years old, but we can make other evaluations," said Conn, whose record is 100-37. "You can see how they respond to stress situations."

Conn understands other coaches and programs are just as dedicated to the game. That is one reason Grayson can stamp out players who are fit to play at Alabama and Georgia, among other colleges in the SEC. The Rams play high-level opponents most every week, and the competition is invaluable to the grooming of players.

"High school football in Georgia is second to none," Conn said.

He will have a player who is second to none in 2012. Robert Nkemdiche is a senior and a defensive end. He is 6-foot-4½,

270 pounds, and runs a 4.5-second 40-yard dash. He is regarded as the top high school player in the country, but the SEC did not get him, the ACC did. Nkemdiche is going to Clemson, which has a reputation for developing standout defensive linemen.

The state of Georgia also has the player ranked No. 2 nationally by recruiting services, Troup linebacker Reuben Foster. The *Atlanta Journal-Constitution*'s Michael Carvell reported in April 2012 that one hundred of Georgia's high school juniors had already been offered Division I scholarships.

Here are two other stories about the passion of high school football in the South.

Mark Lewis, who was named executive vice president for championships and alliances of the NCAA in April, played football at Clarke Central High School in Athens, Georgia. It was a tradition for the players to lift weights at 10:00 a.m. on Christmas morning. There was full participation.

And there is this: In a regular-season away game while Lewis was at Clarke, the placekicker missed an extra point. The rest of the team thought the kicker should walk back to Athens or ride with his parents. He was not allowed on the bus for losing focus.

Clarke had won the game, 69–0.

And this: When Lewis flew to Montana to see his in-laws, he and his wife drove by a football stadium. "That's a pretty nice high school stadium," Lewis said.

"That's the college stadium," his wife said.

"That's part of the difference in the South," said Lewis, who is the son of former Georgia Tech head coach Bill Lewis. "Colleges in the South benefit from the importance of football at the high school level. It helps the SEC to be in the backyard of these high schools and their communities."

Phillip Fulmer, the former Tennessee head coach, who won a national championship in 1998, recruited in Ohio and elsewhere in the Midwest because Tennessee does not typically produce an abundance of high school Division I prospects.

"You have to be careful when you say the South has better football, and better this and better that," Fulmer said. "There are at least twenty elite programs in Ohio, not just at Massillon. You go up to Cleveland and Toledo and you will find good programs there, too."

Fulmer thought another moment about the idea that the South is more stocked with talent than the schools in the Big Ten footprint.

"Let me just say, and I studied this, there are more prospects in Dade and Broward County combined in south Florida than there are in Tennessee, Arkansas, and Kentucky combined. Maybe just say the South has more players."

Urban Meyer, who coached at Florida for six seasons and now has to recruit against the SEC as the Ohio State coach, remembered back to a 2006 SEC coaches' meeting when he told the room, "This is the best conference in the country . . . it's not even close." He had been in the league one season.

"It's population shift, it's high school football, it's a commitment by the SEC schools to hire the best coaches and recruit the best players," Meyer said at the Chick-fil-A Charity Golf Tournament in April 2012.

The South has more players and the SEC goes and gets them. The schools in the SEC recruit hard in a five-hour radius from their school. With plenty of players to choose from, you have to fight to sign them. It is not subtle, either.

When the new Ohio State coach (Meyer) unleashed his staff on the Big Ten, the criticism of the ex-SEC coach and his methods was blistering. Players who had committed to other Big Ten schools signed with the Buckeyes after Meyer contacted them. Recruits saw that Ohio State was stabilized following the scandal under former coach Jim Tressel, and Meyer opened a door for high school seniors to reconsider the Buckeyes.

Meyer never apologized. Six players who had committed to Big Ten schools and two who had committed to Notre Dame were persuaded to sign with the Buckeyes.

" 'Well, we're pissed because you went after guys who were committed,' " Meyer told high school football coaches at a convention, referring to comments made by Michigan State coach Mark Dantonio and Wisconsin coach Bret Bielema. "Yep, and you know what, I've got nine guys who better go do it again. Do it a little harder next time. Do it a little harder."

It is the SEC way of growing a program. If the player is worth the sweat and shows interest, recruit until the bitter end.

"The SEC recruits in a fanatical sort of way," recruiting analyst Tom Lemming said. "There are no easy teams to beat out. I would say more than half of the best recruiters in college football are in the SEC. It is personality and work ethic.

"You know what it is, too? These SEC coaches don't hire their buddies. They hire guys who can coach and recruit. You better not be just a coach. You better be able to get players, too."

The SEC not only grows and grabs some of the best talent, sometimes it can keep it from the NFL, if only for a short while.

In a bowling alley in January 2004 near the Auburn campus, the Auburn running backs Carnell "Cadillac" Williams and Ronnie Brown considered all the fun they were having as college students. They were bowling, their favorite pastime, and they looked at each other and wondered why they had to surrender this fun for playbooks and the vise grip of the NFL.

They were marquee backs, one swift and elusive, the other a locomotive, and the NFL beckoned. Both could be millionaires with the April 2004 draft, but the more they deliberated, the more they thought the NFL could rest on the shelf for another season while they played SEC football.

Williams and Brown talked themselves into staying. They were supposed to be rivals for attention and rivals for opportunities in the Auburn offense. But why not have some more fun? A new offensive coordinator was coming in, and this could be a special season.

It was a special season all right. Auburn went 13-0. The Tigers did not get a chance to win a national championship that season because they started too low in the polls and could not jump past unbeatens Southern Cal and Oklahoma. Brown and Williams did not play in the National Championship Game, but a few years later, while they were in the NFL, both looked back and said they felt fulfilled by their college careers because they stayed in the SEC one more season and felt the thrill one last time.

Now that the caretakers of the BCS have pointed college football toward a four-team play-off and the SEC has grown into Goliath, it will be impossible to keep an undefeated SEC team like 2004 Auburn out of the national championship tournament. The SEC has too much steam to be left out of anything, which brings us to the epic quote, delivered in 2009 by Ellis Johnson, the former assistant coach at South Carolina, to Joe Person of the *State* newspaper. Johnson was asked about escalating salaries in college football and the role of the Knight Commission, which advocates fiscal restraint.

"We don't play the Knight Commission and we don't compete against people that have that theory. We compete in the SEC," Johnson said. "You get in the left lane and go slow in the SEC, they'll run over you."

CHAPTER 4

BUILDING AND REBUILDING LSU

There was a fringe benefit to playing for LSU coach Nick Saban, something valuable to a couple of his players in addition to winning games and getting trained for the NFL. The coach had a pond with fish and he seemed much too busy to snatch those fish out of the water himself. So Mike Clayton, an LSU wide receiver, and Marcus Spears, an LSU defensive end, would make their way around the back of Saban's big house on Highland Road in Baton Rouge and drop lines into the coach's pond and fish.

"Me and Marcus didn't throw nothing back," Clayton said. "We kept them fish."

Clayton was from south Baton Rouge and Spears was from the Bottom, a poorer area of Baton Rouge, and the idea of fishing at the manor of an LSU coach seemed so preposterous if you understood the history between south Baton Rouge, the Bottom, and LSU. Clayton and Spears would never have fished in the pond of an LSU football coach before 2000. Peed in it? Yes, they would have done that.

LSU was mistrusted in some parts of town. The football coach represented a hierarchy at LSU that did not blend with south Baton

Rouge, Clayton said. The coaches were not racist, but their hands seemed tied by politics. Was it accurate? Were there politics? It doesn't matter. That's the way the Claytons of 1415 Barkley Drive saw it and that's what mattered.

When LSU coach Gerry DiNardo, who was regarded as a skilled recruiter, did not show any interest in recruiting Mike Clayton, a star wide receiver from south Baton Rouge, the rift between the neighborhood and the LSU campus grew wider. The Claytons had issues with the politics at LSU, which is to say they thought a good-old-boy element still lurked there when Mike was met with a cold shoulder by DiNardo. If Florida State and Bobby Bowden could recruit him hard, why couldn't his hometown school? The Claytons thought the worst of LSU.

When DiNardo was fired and Saban was hired in late November 1999, LSU began to recruit Clayton, but Saban started the chase from a hole. The hardest thing was not getting in the front door; it was getting through the barbed wire of emotions. Clayton lived in a nice neighborhood with manicured yards, modest but neatly kept homes. What the heck was so objectionable in this neighborhood that it took LSU so long to get in line and recruit a star?

Clayton, who attended Christian Life Academy, already had his bag half packed for Florida State. The heck with LSU. The kids from the Bottom or south Baton Rouge never thought they got a fair shake at LSU, so they were always looking elsewhere first, Clayton said.

"I never got one letter until Saban and his staff got on campus," Clayton said. "Jimbo [Saban assistant coach Jimbo Fisher] would come watch me play basketball, and I would show off for him."

The Claytons let Saban in the front door. "The neighborhood was going, 'What are you doing talkin' to LSU? You know how things can go there,'" Clayton said. "A lot of guys just went to Alcorn, or one of the other HBCUs. We saw too many of our guys go to LSU and then transfer."

Saban, who was in his first season as head coach at LSU, made his pitch to the Claytons. He was earnest, like a man selling Bibles out of the trunk of his car. He talked about college being a forty-year decision, not a four-year decision. He talked about life after football. You could go to your hometown school and come back after the NFL and own shares in a bank, own a clothing store, own real estate. There would be roots.

When the coach was finished vending LSU, Milton Clayton, Mike's father, tried to put his feelings in a gentlemanly sort of way to Saban: "There are politics at LSU, Coach. Things go on. Sometimes the best players don't play."

"There will be no politics," Saban said. "Not as long as I'm here."

Well, how many coaches had said that before only to let politics creep into the locker room, into the meeting room, into the coach's ear? A kid from the South Baton Rouge Rams, among the elite of the Pop Warner football programs, was just asking to be trashed if he believed this blather.

"Don't be sorry, Mike," some of the neighbors told him. "Go to Florida State, go to Miami, go anyplace but *there*." Years of mistrust were barking back at Clayton, and perceptions are hard to tear down. LSU had been one of the last SEC schools to embrace black players. The Claytons were not indicting the whole campus, but they were suspicious, as black folks have learned with justification to be suspicious.

Many LSU fans will likely scoff at Clayton's assertion that as late as 2000 racial prejudices affected the makeup of the Tigers' rosters. Clayton scoffs back at those who think sports is color-blind and that winning overrides all racism.

"Just the other day I'm on the golf course in Tampa, and this white guy rolls by in his cart and says to his friend, 'Hey, look at that nigger playing golf,' " Clayton said. "That's the day we still live in. Some people look at color. It's still not gone."

Clayton already knew the way to Tallahassee and FSU. It wasn't hard. Straight down Barkley, hang a right on Perkins, follow that to I-10, and then a straight shot east. Warrick Dunn of Baton Rouge took that route and played for a national champion at FSU and was an all-American.

Clayton scratched Miami off his recruiting list because on his visit there with Spears, another top-shelf recruit from south Baton Rouge, they found South Beach too raucous and too tempting. "All kinds of stuff going on there," Clayton said.

There was still time to decide before the February 8 signing date, but Clayton thought maybe he should give Saban a chance. Clayton liked Saban, the son of a gasoline-station operator from West Virginia. Florida State was still Clayton's top choice, but a window had opened for LSU, or was it a hole opening in a fence that had been built up between a neighborhood and a school?

On the night of December 29, 2000, Clayton and Spears, who was considered by some the top high school tight end in the country, were sitting in a restaurant in Dallas before they were to play in a high school all-American game. On the restaurant's television, LSU was playing Georgia Tech in the Chick-fil-A Bowl in Atlanta.

A black quarterback, not a white quarterback, flashed across the screen and was making plays. Rohan Davey was taking snaps ahead of Josh Booty, the white quarterback, a Louisiana legend from Evangel Christian. Davey led the Tigers to a win with a strong second-half performance.

Clayton and Spears looked at each other. "What just happened?"

Maybe Saban could override the politics, after all. A black quarterback was allowed to be the star of the game they were watching on TV. It had happened before at LSU with Herb Tyler (1995–98), a black quarterback who shone, but Clayton saw a black quarterback in competition with a white quarterback. The black quarterback scooted ahead; he was allowed to scoot ahead.

In that Dallas restaurant, the Baton Rouge boys started doing something preposterous. They started recruiting for LSU. A south Baton Rouge kid and a kid from the Bottom, who would have stuck their fingers in a light socket before selling for LSU, became salesmen for the Tigers. Perhaps the place wasn't so bad after all. They worked on the high school players in Dallas at the all-star game who had still not made up their minds where to go to college. In all, Clayton said, six players in that game went to LSU.

"He meant what he said about there not being politics anymore," Clayton said of Saban. "You could tell on the television that night. What Rohan did changed some people's minds."

Spears flipped to LSU. He was all set to follow Jeremy Shockey and Bubba Franks at Miami and be the Hurricanes' next all-American tight end. LSU wasn't in the picture for the longest time, he said, and then he decided Saban was the real deal.

"It was, who is your daddy? Who did your daddy play for? How much money did they give?" said Spears. "Nick got there and he could have cared less whose daddy played there."

Clayton signed with LSU. So did Spears. Marquise Hill, a star defensive end from New Orleans, bought into the Tigers, and so did Rudy Niswanger, a star offensive lineman from Monroe. Andrew Whitworth, a lineman also from Monroe, the sixth-best offensive line prospect in the country, signed with LSU. Saban also signed Ben Wilkerson, an all-American lineman from Hemphill, Texas.

In 2003, LSU (13-1) won a national championship. That 2001 class—headlined by Clayton and Spears, two Baton Rouge stars who had sworn they would not play for the Tigers—was the core of the first LSU team to win a title since 1958.

That 2003 title team is not part of the string of six straight national champions from the SEC, but that team revived LSU, which had been knocking on the door to a national championship for forty-odd years, but never crossed the threshold. It had always been a mystery why LSU, with so many talented players in the state—and with Texas and its rich vein of talent nearby—had not won more national championships. Some of it had to do with the dominant teams of Alabama and Bear Bryant, who just shoved the rest of the SEC into a corner. But Bryant was dead twenty years. What was LSU waiting for? Saban?

The perception before Saban, Spears said, was that LSU wanted to recruit nationally. It did not work hard enough to harvest the talent in-state, and players, such as Dunn, found it easy to leave. Spears said Saban had poked around Louisiana, talked to people, and discovered how deep the talent pool was in the state before he took the job at LSU in November 1999.

"When Nick took that job, he knew that schools that are successful, and who are the only major program in their state, can win if they lock the doors and keep the best players for their program," said Spears, who became a first-team all-American in 2004 and was a first-round draft pick of the Dallas Cowboys. "His biggest pitch was that we have enough guys in this state to get done what we want to get done. The core guys in that class of 2001, except Ben Wilkerson, who was from Texas, were from Louisiana. He talked about Louisiana pride."

The 2000 Tigers, Saban's first team, finished 8-4. They beat

No. 11 Tennessee and they beat Alabama. That gave the LSU fandom a sense that Saban, with players left over from the 3-8 1999 team, could take somebody else's players and win. The next question that had to be asked caused statewide anticipation: What could he do with his own players?

Charles Thomas, a defensive end from Baton Rouge, a holdover from the previous coaching regime, said Saban started paying attention to details around the program. The new coach had a worn chain-link fence that was covered in faded green canvas taken down at the Ponderosa, the practice fields, and replaced with a freshly painted wood fence.

Thomas said the overflow locker room under the stadium, the large closet for the walk-ons, was painted and given some of the starch that was reserved for the scholarship locker room.

"The fence and the locker room spoke volumes to what he was trying to do," said Thomas, who had been invited as a walk-on by the previous head coach, Gerry DiNardo. "Coach Saban was paying attention to little details; he wouldn't let anything slide by. Expectations started to grow, and it was that attention to the small things that impressed me. It wasn't just his playbook that made him a good coach. He sent a message that we're serious about football around here."

No more mutinies occurred around the football program as with DiNardo. After some particularly brutal two-a-day practices under DiNardo in 1995, the veteran players confronted the coach in the locker room, but when the rest of the team hesitated in backing them, DiNardo took control and ordered the players to the practice fields. A few days later, after more two-a-days in the searing heat, players stood around receiver Eddie Kennison's truck in the parking lot and wanted to march on DiNardo's office. They backed down again.

The Tigers were 10-2 in 1996, then 9-3, then started to sputter.

They went 4-7, then 3-8, and the new chancellor, Mark Emmert, knew there had to be a change.

In early November 1999, the decision had already been made to fire DiNardo, so athletic director Joe Dean and three other members of a search committee flew to Dallas, where they were picked up at the airport by Gil Brandt, the former Dallas Cowboys executive. They drove to Brandt's office and he pulled out his ten-year study of coaching hires and what the qualifications of the next coach should be. The LSU group also hired Chuck Neinas and his search firm to work up a list of candidates.

Butch Davis, who was the head coach of Miami, was one of the candidates. The LSU contingent flew to south Florida in the middle of November and interviewed Davis for four hours. They wanted him. They all knew it on the plane ride back to Baton Rouge.

"We offered him the job," Dean said.

Davis asked for time to consider the offer. One of the people pushing Davis to accept the LSU job was Tommy Moffitt, the Miami strength and conditioning coach who would go on to become the LSU strength and conditioning coach and work with two national championship teams.

Two days after the interview, Davis called Dean and declined the offer for a good reason.

"I can win this league I'm in now," Davis told Dean. "That league you're in is a monster."

LSU kept searching. They flew to Chicago and met with Glen Mason, the University of Minnesota coach. Dean sized up Mason as wanting to be offered the job on the spot, and as a coach not being too enthralled with the interview process. LSU was not ready to jump with Mason, the way it was with Davis. While LSU deliberated, Mason withdrew from consideration.

In the meantime, Brandt flew to Oregon to meet with Dennis Erickson, who was the Oregon State coach, but LSU did not interview Erickson. Brandt was also high on the Michigan State coach, Nick Saban, but the LSU search team did not get around to Saban right away.

To the list of names of coaches the LSU search team wanted to talk to they added Mark Richt, the Florida State offensive coordinator. But before they could set up an interview with Richt, Dean got a call from Sean Tuohy, a former basketball player at Ole Miss and the stepfather of Michael Oher, the Baltimore Ravens offensive lineman and subject of the movie *The Blind Side*.

Tuohy asked Dean if LSU would talk to Tuohy's friend the agent Jimmy Sexton, who represented Saban. Dean agreed. They set up a meeting for lunch with Saban at Sexton's house in Germantown, Tennessee, in the Memphis area, at noon on a Saturday, and the LSU search team flew north to Olive Branch, Mississippi. Tuohy picked up the men at the airport. The group included chancellor Mark Emmert, Charlie Weems, the chairman of the board, and search committee members Stanley Jacobs, Richard Gill, and Dean.

It was one of the most important interviews in the history of SEC football. Saban was hired and has won three national championships in the SEC. He rebuilt LSU into a national contender and has done the same with Alabama. What if he had stayed in the Big Ten?

"We didn't know if Nick Saban could coach," Dean said. "He had been around .500 his first four years at Michigan State, and then nine and two. He had been an assistant most of his career. We just didn't know.

"We do now."

In Sexton's home, Emmert heard Saban's game plan for the job and was fascinated by his intellect and his approach to the game.

"He had done extraordinary research and given really deep thought to what was possible at LSU," Emmert said. "LSU had not won a championship in fifty years, and people were still talking about Billy Cannon's run on Halloween like it happened the day before. It had been a long time since the last national championship.

"Nick recognized that Louisiana led the nation in NFL players per capita, and he had a plan to win a championship."

Before Saban could finish his audition, the LSU chancellor just came out with it. "I want you to be my football coach," Emmert told Saban.

"I didn't wait to talk to my board. It was as clear as anything I have ever done," Emmert said.

Emmert wanted Saban, and it was a shock when the LSU CEO stepped out of the SEC family to make the hire. Ron Higgins, a reporter for the *Commercial Appeal* in Memphis, has researched the hiring of SEC coaches and found that the vast majority of the head coaches had ties to the school where they were hired.

The LSU contingent got up to leave, and Emmert told Sexton, "Jimmy, this is the easiest deal you are ever going to make. Tell me a number and we'll do it."

The number was approximately $1.2 million, double what Di-Nardo was being paid. Emmert was not going to leave the door open for Michigan State to make a counteroffer. And that was what separated the SEC and the Big Ten. Money. The SEC was the first conference, generally, to spend big money on head coaches and then assistant coaches. Jeremy Foley, the athletic director at Florida, did that when he hired Steve Spurrier. Emmert and Dean were paying a premium for Saban as well.

Saban's hiring and new riches created two issues. Emmert had to return to campus and calm his faculty senate, which was outraged by the salary given to a football coach. The LSU athletic department had operated in the black under Dean, a former business executive, and one year when faculty was to go without pay raises, the athletic department under Dean's watch provided the university with $2 million for raises. That still did not calm the teachers on campus, and Emmert took some flak.

Emmert also had to explain to the fandom why he hired a no-name from a Yankee school.

Before the decision was announced, "my wife and Terry Saban walked into TJ Ribs and they [the restaurant] were having a contest about who would be the next LSU coach," Emmert said. "There was a list of names posted. Nick's name wasn't on the list."

Emmert gave the new coach more than money and name recognition in the Bayou. He gave Saban access to some of the best high school football talent in the country and access to some of the most passionate fans in college football. They were penned up like Mike the Tiger, always trailing Bear Bryant's Tide or Pat Dye's Tigers, or the Vols, or Spurrier's Gators. They would adore the coach who came through the door and won. And Saban won.

Saban, who had been the coach for five seasons at Michigan State, said LSU needed a football facility out at the Ponderosa, the wide patch of land where the team practiced. Emmert agreed. The Tigers would leave the stadium in buses every afternoon for practice across Nicholson Drive, and that was inefficient. The staff and coaches needed space for offices, an indoor practice facility, and room to host recruits. Saban helped design the building, but left to coach the Miami Dolphins before it was built.

Saban said the graduation rate of athletes—not just football players—could be improved with a better learning environment, and he found out the hard way about LSU's deficiencies in the classroom. He was ambushed on the recruiting trail in New Orleans his first day on the job when parents asked him why they would ever send their kids to LSU, which had a miserable graduation rate for football players.

Saban called Emmert and fumed, "Why didn't you tell me we had the worst graduation rate in the SEC?"

"If that's true, I didn't know it," said Emmert, who had been on the job just five months. The two men agreed it had to be fixed.

"The day we played in the National Championship Game against Oklahoma, which would have been January 2004, I was invited to write an op-ed piece in the *New York Times*," Emmert said. "That doesn't happen very often for LSU. I was able to talk about the misperception that the South is all about football when we have all these great things going on academically. Football helped deliver that message."

In the fall of 2000, Saban approached Richard Manship, a booster and CEO of Capital City Press and a local television station, and asked him to lead the fund-raising for the academic center. They raised more than $14 million in private funds to build the Cox Communications Academic Center for Student-Athletes, which came online November 15, 2002. The center is available to all students at LSU.

The spigot was opened. Players poured into the pipeline of talent at LSU. Clayton, Spears, and others started recruiting players for Saban and for his successor, Les Miles. According to recruiting analyst Tom Lemming, LSU's recruiting classes were in the top ten in seven of the last eight years. LSU won another title in 2007, under Miles, and played for the championship in 2011, losing to, of all people, Saban, who was now the coach at Alabama.

"It's on a roll now at LSU," Spears said. "Our class got it over the hump."

Saban left LSU in 2004 for a job with the Miami Dolphins, and Miles was hired from Oklahoma State, which was like jumping on a moving merry-go-round. The team was composed of players Miles recruited and players Saban had recruited, and there were expectations to stay up to speed. Miles did that. He won with Saban's players for several years and then his own players. He was viewed as quirky for chewing grass and for all the adventures and misadventures near the end of a few games, but he was a good coach. The Tigers were 11-2 in 2005 and played in the SEC Championship Game Miles's first season. They were 11-2 in 2006 and crushed Notre Dame in the Sugar Bowl (41–14) in his second season.

In 2007, LSU was 12-2 and won the national championship (the Tigers like to say they were undefeated in regulation; they lost two games in triple overtime). It took some good fortune for Miles's third team to win that title and help a good guy get his hands on the trophy. Undefeated West Virginia was stunned by archrival Pitt, 13–9, to open the door (see chapter 7) for the Tigers, who slipped into the National Championship Game and thumped No. 1 Ohio State, 38–24. No one doubted the Tigers national championship credentials after that game.

The 2007 LSU team included Saban recruits defensive tackle Glenn Dorsey and safety Craig Steltz, who were all-Americans. Offensive lineman Herman Johnson, defensive back Chevis Jackson, and linebacker Ali Highsmith were all-SEC players. Running back Jacob Hester rushed for 1,103 yards in 2007, and superb wide receiver Early Doucet could not be guarded by Alabama in a win in Tuscaloosa. Defensive tackle Marlon Favorite was another Saban guy. So, too, was center Brett Helms, along with defensive tackle Claude Wroten.

But Miles called them "my guys" and artfully blended his own recruits with the Saban holdovers to produce an exciting team that played on the edge all season with their fun-filled head coach.

Miles reloaded after Saban and the Tigers finished the 2011 regular season 12-0 and blew out Georgia, 42–10, in the SEC Championship Game. The wins included a 9–6 victory over Saban and Alabama in Tuscaloosa, but the Tide got more than even in the National Championship Game with a 21–0 victory to spoil the Miles ride.

The Tigers have the makings of a top five team again in 2012, which is all Miles's doing, but there is no denying the program was put on the rails again by Saban with his player evaluation and disdain for the usual politics of the Bayou. This is a heyday in Baton Rouge, just as in the fifties when Billy Cannon won a Heisman Trophy and the state was teeming with talent, all destined for LSU. The Tigers won the national championship in 1958 behind Cannon, who is still considered the greatest player in the school's history.

Clayton insists that Saban's LSU "guys" are now Miles's LSU guys. Given a chance to paint Miles as just living off Saban's rebuilding of the LSU brand, Clayton said he has talked to too many Tigers who have played for Miles and insist he is a sensational leader and a good coach.

"I know the players who played under him and what they say about him, and that's all I need to hear," Clayton said. "They respond to him. They are on the right track. He has a handle on his team. He gets the most out of them and he is a great leader. Hands down he has done that. I believe that's why he has been successful; it's how he leads."

Miles, and the coaches who follow him, no doubt benefit from Saban's work. But it was not easy keeping things on the rails once Saban recruited that class of 2001. He had to work to keep the players there as he instituted his system of player evaluation, which was to judge height, weight, and speed and get players matched up with their best position, not their favorite position. Spears, for one, almost left in the spring of 2002. He wanted to be a tight end and catch passes and score touchdowns. He wanted to have some of the spotlight, but Saban told Spears after his freshman season in 2001 he was being moved to defensive end.

"I'm leaving," Spears told Saban in a meeting.

"Why?"

"I want to play tight end, it's the best thing for my future," Spears said.

"Let me show you something." Saban reached into his drawer and pulled out a folder with the salaries of NFL players by position. Defensive ends made more money than tight ends.

"Coach," Spears said, "I am going to be the best defensive end I can be."

When Saban came to Corey Webster's house in Louisiana after Webster's freshman year to also talk about a position change, Webster and his father wanted to throw Saban out of the house on his head. The coach was proposing moving Webster from receiver to cornerback. Webster had known only offense as an all-state player in high school. Saban was crazy, they thought.

"He saw me play basketball and how I stayed in front of people," Webster said. "Coach Saban said, 'You have to trust me.' He said I am going to be a corner that is all-SEC and all-American and that I will never look back at it.

"I'm not going to lie. We still weren't thrilled about it after that conversation. We just looked at each other and said he is just saying all this stuff. No way I should switch. He made two trips to my house to try and talk to us about it.

"And everything he said was exactly what happened."

Webster was a two-time first-team all-American. In 2008, he signed a five-year, $43.5 million deal with $20 million guaranteed with the New York Giants. Webster has two Super Bowl rings.

"When he came from Michigan State, he said he was going to bring the graduation rate up, and we're going to build this kind of academic center, and do this with academics," Webster said. "And all of those things happened at LSU. The graduation rate went up twenty percent when he was there.

"He still calls me; I call him."

Saban's follow-through worked for Clayton, too. That four-year decision for Clayton was a forty-year decision, just as the coach said. Clayton owns shares in a bank in Louisiana and owns real estate in Baton Rouge. LSU had been a distant place for him, even though he had walked on campus plenty of times as a kid. The school helped him as a football player and as a businessman, and the bitterness he once felt has been swept away by goodwill.

Clayton and Spears became so comfortable with Saban that they would walk to his house and disappear through the bushes to the backyard. Clayton and Spears would pull fish out of that pond, and who cared if it was an NCAA violation, or not. The two kids—one from south Baton Rouge, the other from the Bottom—were throwing lines into a millionaire's pond and getting away with it. There was no fence to keep them out. There was no fence to keep any of the Louisiana kids out. There was only a fence to keep Louisiana players in. Nick Saban had torn down one fence and built another.

CHAPTER 5

"THE BADDEST MEN ON THE PLANET"

Ryan Pugh, the center on Auburn's 2010 national championship team, did not get drafted by an NFL team. He lifted enough weights, ran enough sprints, and looked at enough film, but he did something wrong and knew exactly what it was. The weights, the sprints, and the film could not trump it.

He took a wrong turn coming out of high school in Birmingham, Alabama.

He should have gone North or West or East. He stayed South. A lot of offensive linemen who have played in the SEC have made the same mistake.

"When the NFL draft came around in 2011, me and some other guys on the offensive line were saying to each other, 'Why didn't we go to another conference coming out of high school, why did we pick the SEC?' " Pugh said. "Our film would have looked a lot better; we would have had fewer injuries."

He smiled and shook his head from side to side. "We had to pick the SEC, the conference with the baddest men on the planet on the other side of the ball from us. Why didn't we choose the big, slow guy from the Big Ten to block, or the skinny guy from the Pac-10?"

The baddest men on the planet, as far as Pugh is concerned, play on the defensive line in the SEC. They bring mayhem and disorder, and they have inflicted cruelties on the offenses of the Big Ten, Big 12, and Pac-10 the last six years, not to mention their brethren blockers in the SEC. Indeed, the most significant contribution to the SEC's run of six national championships is not the 60-yard run by the tailback, the spiraling touchdown pass, or the sudden drama of a kick return for a touchdown. It is the harm brought by the SEC marauders, those bad men, who come off the edge or up the middle. They have stuffed the run game, pestered your quarterback, and blown up game plans in the National Championship Game. The faster a defensive lineman gets to the quarterback, the less work it means for the back end of the defense.

Here are three plays that should start any highlight reel of the SEC's six-pack of championships.

Scene One: January 2007. Ohio State vs. Florida. Florida's Jarvis Moss sacks Ohio State's Heisman Trophy winner, quarterback Troy Smith, and forces a fumble just before halftime. Derrick Harvey snatches the loose ball, and Florida, already leading 27–14, has the ball at the Buckeyes' 5-yard line. The turnover led to a touchdown and a 34–14 lead, and the Gators won in a rout, 41–14.

Scene Two: January 2010. Texas vs. Alabama. Alabama's Marcell Dareus steams around from the back side and buries a shoulder pad into the back of Texas quarterback Colt McCoy in the National Championship Game for the 2009 season. McCoy is knocked out of the game by the hit, and the Crimson Tide beat the Longhorns, 37–21, for the fourth straight SEC national championship.

Scene Three: January 2011. Oregon vs. Auburn. Oregon had

a fourth-and-goal at the Auburn 1, down 19–11 in the third quarter of the 2010 season National Championship Game. The Tigers' Nick Fairley burrows his way into the backfield on the left side, and the defense swarms over the Ducks' Kenjon Barner, who is stopped short of the goal line. Auburn wins on a late field goal, 22–19.

Ohio State's Smith, Texas's McCoy, and Oregon quarterback Darron Thomas were the richest men in the graveyard in those title games. They had all this blazing speed at their hands, wonderful talent to hand off to or throw to, but they were dead rich men because the SEC defensive linemen wouldn't be consistently blocked.

It is no wonder the turning point in three National Championship Games came from the SEC defensive line. Since the 2007 NFL draft, the SEC has had fifty-four defensive linemen drafted. The ACC, by comparison, has had forty.

It is not just quantity, but quality. Since the 2007 draft, thirteen defensive linemen from the SEC have gone in the first round, while the ACC has had six.

You don't have to tell Pugh about SEC defensive linemen. He was nose to nose with Dareus in the Iron Bowl, and he had to deal with Fairley in practice.

"I'll tell you one thing, you knew who you were up against in the SEC. First-round picks," Pugh said. "And you responded to it. You respected who was against you on Saturday all across this conference."

You could take a team photo of all the dominant defensive linemen in the SEC in this six-year streak, but the picture frame would have to be the size of a bus. Derrick Harvey, Ray McDonald, Carlos Dunlap, and Jarvis Moss of Florida. Glenn Dorsey, Drake Nevis, Sam Montgomery, Michael Brockers, and Tyson Jackson of LSU. Marcell Dareus and Terrence Cody of Alabama. Peria Jerry and Jerrell Powe of Ole Miss. Fletcher Cox and Pernell McPhee of Mississippi State. Melvin Ingram of South Carolina. Nick Fairley of Auburn and Jake Bequette of Arkansas. Quentin Moses, Charles Johnson, and Geno Atkins of Georgia. Those are just some of the names of the marauders from the last six years. Alabama plays a 3-4 defense, but lining up on the edge to rush the passer are defensive ends called linebackers, such as Courtney Upshaw and Rolando McClain and Dont'a Hightower.

Get ready for the next all-world defensive linemen from the SEC: South Carolina's Jadeveon Clowney, a sophomore in 2012. He will be the defensive end opposite another high-round 2013 draft pick, Carolina defensive end Devin Taylor. A pipeline stretches from South Carolina to Louisiana and soon into Texas.

"Every week in the SEC, you're usually dealing with a matchup issue somewhere up front," Lane Kiffin, the former Tennessee coach, told Michael Carvell of the *Atlanta Journal-Constitution*. "Out here [in the Pac-12] you don't have as many dominant front sevens and, specifically, defensive linemen. That's not a knock on anyone. That's just studying the NFL draft. The draft will show you that . . . where out here, you get better passing games sometimes with quarterbacks and wide receivers. You get different things in different areas of the country."

The prototype SEC defensive end has long arms to get his hands on the offensive lineman before the blocker can get his hands on the defender. The SEC defensive end can reach past the outside shoulder of the blocker for leverage. He has an explosive step up the field and can weigh 260 pounds and still play outside. He can play the run, but get after the passer, too.

Here's something else. Defensive linemen are so good in the SEC, the offense knows only one tactic at the point of attack with a run play: a double-team block. It takes six hundred pounds, or two blockers, to move three hundred pounds. It really does. Over the years that has helped create a physical conference. Steve Spurrier's Fun N Gun offense of the nineties at Florida brought a different culture of offense to the SEC, and the passing game was expanded in some programs, but pass-first did not take root as it did in other conferences. Spurrier was innovative with his matchup passing game, and he ushered in an era of more versatile football, but the game is still won up the middle in the SEC, from the inside out.

It is big people beating up little people.

"It has always been a very physical conference because of the size of the defensive linemen and the speed of the linebackers and the defensive backs," said Phil Savage, the executive director of the Senior Bowl, former general manager of the Cleveland Browns, and college scout and assistant coach. "Population shift is part of it. There is a cultural piece somewhere that has to do with the actual size of these players. You could point to every SEC school, and each one has had a big-time defensive lineman at one time or another."

The SEC's identity on the defensive line did not just start with LSU's Brockers and Alabama's Dareus. The long line of stellar defensive ends includes Georgia's Marcus Stroud, David Pollack, and Richard Seymour, and Florida's Gerard Warren and Trace Armstrong, and Alabama's Eric Curry and John Copeland, and on and on.

The SEC game has turned into double-teaming gang-up on the play side because of the conference's collection of all-American defensive linemen. Single-blocking in the SEC? You just don't see much of it because of the strength and skill of the defensive linemen. Blocking a three-technique in the SEC has to be the hardest block in football. That three-hundred-pound tackle, a force of nature and training, can control a gap, but he can also rush the quarterback.

The blocker who has to deal with that bird has a grueling assignment. Glenn Dorsey of LSU was a three-technique; Alabama's Dareus would be another; Auburn's Fairley another. These guys were strong and agile, and the good ones go high in the NFL draft. Dareus was picked No. 3 overall and Fairley No. 13 in the 2011 draft. Dorsey was picked No. 5 overall in the 2008 draft.

"The Nick Saban/Bill Belichick philosophy, from when I was with the Browns with them, was to be strong down the middle defensively, and it carries across the line to the offense, as well," Savage said.

He added that what the scouts want in the defensive lineman— and they can find it across the country, but more of it in the SEC—is:

On the inside, physical size, strength, and explosiveness. The athletic ability to be able to move. A competitive nature, the instincts to make a play. When a guy has all those things, he is a first round pick.

Ideally, the defensive end is going to have some length to them, in terms of height and long arms. They are going to have the first-step quickness to get off the spot, but then an ability to make the countermove, that athletic ability to change gears, spin inside, use their hands. The hand use is something the colleges have gotten better at. It is really refined in the pro game. Hand-to-hand combat in terms of pass rush is important.

Defensive linemen in the SEC are why third downs can expose a quarterback as skilled enough or too shaky to have an impact. The young quarterbacks in the SEC have to *feel* the rush of the line and still keep their eyes downfield with the assault under way, which is difficult and takes time to master. It's why most freshman and junior college quarterbacks, who have succeeded in high school or juco ball, need some seasoning and do not immediately succeed in the SEC. Not only must they contend with the defensive linemen, but the crowds, especially on the road.

"When you get to third down in an SEC stadium, and it's a game on the road, the ground shakes," said Chris Leak, the quarterback of Florida's 2006 championship team. "Then you have these guys coming at you, and that's as close to the NFL as you will get in college. I remember one season where I was following the SEC, and the Tennessee defensive line had Albert Haynesworth and John Henderson [2001]. I remember Glenn Dorsey was an all-American at LSU. There were others, a lot of others."

It is no wonder, then, that the SEC has not signed its share of blue-chip high school quarterbacks or routinely spits out quarterbacks with gaudy statistics who deceive the NFL scouts and get picked on draft day. The defensive lines of the SEC persuade QBs to find a safer environment in another league. Statistics are hard to accumulate when it is a problem just setting your feet to throw.

Think about the SEC quarterbacks who have recently succeeded in the NFL. Matthew Stafford of Georgia. Who else? Cam Newton of Auburn might be on his way, but his second season is coming up in 2012. We're going to see if he can hit the curveball, so to speak. He throws a lot of short passes down the hash marks to tight ends for the Panthers.

In this six-year run, some quarterbacks have had good seasons: Tim Tebow won the Heisman at Florida. Leak had a sensational career at Florida and remains underrated for his production. He took the Gators to a national title. Stephen Garcia did well at South Carolina in 2010, but regressed in 2011 and was kicked off the team.

The quarterback who looked primed for an NFL career was Tennessee's Erik Ainge, who had a remarkable quarterback rating of 135.2 his senior season in 2007. He certainly showed his mettle as a quarterback in the SEC, but injuries ruined his chances to be a solid NFL quarterback and forced him to retire.

What is that? Six names over six seasons. That's it. (Jay Cutler of Vanderbilt came out just before the six-season streak of titles.)

So does the SEC go too far in trying to find pass-rushing, run-stuffing bullies who push around quarterbacks? Do they cut corners academically?

Jon Solomon of the *Birmingham News*, who is one of the best reporters covering the Southeastern Conference, unearthed a treasure about SEC defensive linemen to the delight of the Big Ten and other conferences.

In 2011, Solomon reported that the SEC had signed fifty defensive linemen since 2006 who had attended junior college or prep school, presumably because they needed academic help. The Big Ten, meanwhile, had signed nineteen in those years.

In the 2012 recruiting classes, the SEC added four defensive linemen that attended junior college or prep school.

After Florida waxed Ohio State in January 2007 to win the national championship, the Big Ten commissioner, Jim Delany, could not restrain himself. He made an ax-grinding post to the Big Ten website that quickly circulated through the SEC and made its way to the SEC offices in Birmingham. He specifically mentioned SEC defensive linemen:

> *I love speed and the SEC has great speed, especially on the defensive line, but there are appropriate balances when mixing academics and athletics. Each school, as well as each conference, simply must do what fits their mission regardless of what a*

recruiting service recommends. I wish we had six teams among the top ten recruiting classes every year, but winning our way requires some discipline and restraint with the recruitment process. Not every athlete fits athletically, academically, or socially at every university. Fortunately, we have been able to balance our athletic and academic mission so that we can compete successfully and keep faith with our academic standards.

Let's see if the five- and ten-year trend lines hold or whether the recruiting services and talking heads are seeing a new day. We are quite proud of our history and tradition and remain optimistic about the future of Big Ten football.

Charles Bloom, the associate commissioner of the SEC for media, was mowing his grass at his home in Birmingham on the Saturday the Delany item appeared on the Big Ten website. Teddy Greenstein of the *Chicago Tribune* called Bloom for a reaction. Bloom called Mike Slive, the commissioner of the SEC, who was in Lexington, Kentucky, for a swimming and diving meet and then a basketball game later that night. Bloom could almost hear the steam coming from Slive as he read his boss the passage on the Big Ten website.

"Charles, meet me in the office at eight tomorrow, Sunday morning," Slive told Bloom, "we'll work up a response."

Bloom's version of a response was measured; Slive's version was lightning on paper. Bloom succeeded in convincing Slive, usually a mild-mannered sort, that his anger at Delany's remarks might drown out the SEC's message in response.

The war of words did not change that Delany's quarterback, Ohio State's Troy Smith, was bothered throughout the National Championship Game by Florida's array of speed rushers. The loss embarrassed the Buckeyes and the Big Ten because they had claimed

Michigan should have been in the National Championship Game, not the Gators. The Big Ten argument was that Urban Meyer's politicking for Florida caused the Wolverines to be passed over by voters in the final BCS rankings.

"Honestly, we've played a lot better teams than them," Moss, the Florida defensive end, said after the game. "I could name four or five teams in the SEC that could probably compete with them and play the same type of game we did against them."

Delany was part of the BCS cartel (the ACC aside) that would not even discuss Slive's proposal in 2008 for a plus-one model to settle the issue of who would play for the national championship. Slive's proposal, partly a response to undefeated Auburn's being denied a title shot in 2004, was met mostly with stone-cold silence. The ill will toward the SEC stems in part from a perception that the SEC has cheated its way to the top, and Delany has put some weight behind that perception.

"Commissioner Slive does not like Commissioner Delany," said Les Miles, the LSU coach.

The bitterness has lingered. The Big Ten coaches fired away at the SEC in February 2012 when Meyer displayed some SEC-style aggressive recruiting after becoming the Ohio State coach. The Big Ten coaches did not have to fear any reprisals from their commissioner because he has egged them on for years with his sniping at the SEC.

Yes, some high jinks have occurred as the SEC has tried to accumulate defensive linemen. One case resulted in punishment and a firing.

LSU assistant coach D. J. McCarthy was chasing a junior college star named Akiem Hicks, who was playing football at Sacramento (California) City College. Hicks received some transportation and housing other than for his official visit during the recruiting push, which were major violations. He was supposed to play in 2009, but when LSU began the investigation in September 2009, it would not let Hicks get on the field, fearing he was ineligible.

Hicks never played for LSU, and McCarthy was fired following the 2009 season.

The NCAA put LSU on a year's probation, which was during the 2011 season when LSU was climbing to No. 1. It also took away two scholarships. The Tigers avoided more serious penalties by self-reporting the violation and putting some penalties in place before the NCAA took action.

Glenn Guilbeau of Gannett reported that Miles's contract was suddenly in jeopardy, all because of a talented defensive end. A clause in Miles's contract says that if he is fired without cause, he will be due $15 million. But if he is fired after an NCAA probe and sanctions, there will be no buyout.

"That is correct," LSU chancellor Mike Martin told Guilbeau. "NCAA violations negate the buyout." In a twist to the story, Hicks, who ended up playing college ball in Canada, was drafted by none other than the New Orleans Saints in the third round of the 2012 draft.

The recruitment of junior college players has caused the caretakers of college football to lean on schools to be more academically minded when pursuing junior college players. Starting in 2013–14, junior college transfers would need a 2.5 GPA and could count only two physical education credits toward their initial eligibility. It might surprise some of its detractors, but the SEC was behind this legislation from the start and did not fight it.

Todd Grantham, the defensive coordinator at Georgia, said the competition is fierce in the SEC for "big guys who are athletic," which is the definition of what defensive linemen need to be in the conference. Schools will routinely shop down the junior college aisle to sign a defensive lineman, who can be the biggest impact player on the field because the truly good linemen stop the run and bother the quarterback.

"You work more ways to find the good ones," Grantham said. "That means junior college, as well as high school. It is easier to find the offensive lineman; it is not as easy the D-lineman. And there are a lot of junior colleges in the South, which is why we have so many defensive linemen from junior colleges in the SEC."

The SEC is a beacon to defensive linemen. The majority of the good ones who attend SEC schools hail from the South, but others see the fierce play in the SEC and can be imported from other parts of the country. Ronald Powell, a defensive end from Moreno Valley, California, was rated as high as the No. 2 recruit in the country in the 2010 recruiting class. When Pete Carroll left Southern Cal for the Seattle Seahawks, Powell flipped to Florida.

Sharrif Floyd was another highly recruited defensive lineman and played for George Washington High School in Philadelphia. Penn State? No way. He signed with Florida. Dominique Easley was a five-star recruit from Staten Island, New York, and he also signed with Florida in 2010, which was Urban Meyer's last recruiting class with the Gators. Those three defensive linemen, all from out of state, all among the best in the nation, showed the reach and allure of the SEC.

"It's the defensive front sevens in the SEC, that's the difference between the SEC and the other leagues," Meyer said. "The SEC has that reputation of turning out D-linemen. I remember when we recruited those D-linemen from outside the South. They came because they wanted to be part of an SEC defensive line. They told me that. They were among the best players in the country."

In the era of the spread offense, the SEC believes in playing football as it did in the era of the black-and-white television: rock-'em, sock-'em football. Attack with the defensive front and control the line of scrimmage. The SEC gets the biggest and fastest to assault the quarterback.

The SEC not only signs them as recruits, it coaches them. It makes them faster and more explosive.

"If you can't teach them to come off the football; if you can't teach them to play with their hips underneath; if you can't teach them hand and helmet placement and leg drive that comes out of their hips—you can't play defensive line in this league," Miles said. "You can see it every Saturday . . . those teams that got it and those teams that don't."

It's why the defensive line coach is a premium assistant-coaching position in the SEC. The talent a school accumulates needs direction. Miles took his defensive line coach, Brick Haley, from the Chicago Bears.

"If you don't have a great one, you have to hire a great one," Miles said of his D-line coach. "We will always be known on the defensive side for our line. Our corners get drafted, too. You have to have a great corner and a great defensive line in this league. Now you can afford to bring an extra linebacker because that corner can cover. You can bring a safety [on the blitz] and put the other safety in the middle of the field because that corner can cover by himself out there and you help him because there is pressure coming on the quarterback."

The quality defensive lineman makes all the combination defenses possible in the secondary because he is getting to the quarterback before the passer can decipher the coverage. Is it man or zone? Who is blitzing and who is falling off into coverage?

The SEC teams with good defensive linemen do not have to blitz as much because their four linemen can get to the quarterback just as well as the team that rushes four and fires a linebacker on a blitz. Then with teams such as Alabama and LSU, which have good cornerbacks who can play man-to-man, it means their linebackers can stay in the middle of the field to tackle the quarterback when he is flushed out and made to run by the defensive line. Quarterbacks in the SEC do not make as many big-play scrambles. That linebacker can also be the fifth pass rusher, and that means even more pressure on the quarterback.

"In that National Championship Game between Florida and Ohio State, Ohio State may have overlooked the defensive line a little bit," said Ron Zook, who became the Illinois coach in 2007. "We had guys who played fast and played with leverage, and I don't think Ohio State was used to that speed and quickness and guys coming off the edge like that. They weren't the big guys from teams like Michigan; the Florida guys were a little smaller, but they were fast and strong."

The rest of college football has certainly turned out some NFL-caliber defensive linemen the last six seasons. There was B. J. Raji of Boston College, Aaron Maybin of Penn State, Chris Long of Virginia, Jason Pierre-Paul of South Florida, Elvis Dumervil of Louisville, among others. But what separates the SEC is the wave of defensive linemen that come off the bench in the second or third quarter when the starters need a break from the collisions. They are freshman or sophomore backups who were stars in high school and could play in other conferences.

"As far as the depth of the defensive front seven, that's the SEC's advantage," said Mike Johnson, who played on the offensive line for Alabama's 2009 national championship team. "You are going to see teams from other conferences with talent, but it's the guys who are coming in behind the starters who are also four-star players. Other leagues might have one lineup for the front seven. We have backups, and those backups can play multiple roles. We can go two or three deep. The defensive front seven and the offensive line is where you notice the depth in the SEC and don't miss a beat.

"So you can see how we win with a power game. More big people who can play. You can see draft picks come from schools all over the country, but you tell the difference when there is an injury or a guy gets tired. Can you put together a two-deep on the defensive line? The SEC can."

More than a month-long break followed Auburn's win over South Carolina in the SEC Championship Game in 2010 until the National Championship Game with Oregon. The Tigers' offensive line became bored watching the Ducks' defensive line. They asked line coach Jeff Grimes to pop in a tape of Oregon's offensive line.

"That's all it took for us to know we were going to win that game," Pugh said. "We saw their offensive line and we knew they couldn't block us. We just knew they couldn't block us and they didn't." Oregon, which had been averaging 303 yards rushing in the regular season, managed 75 against the Tigers.

The SEC is about to have company again from Florida State when it comes to defensive linemen, just like in the nineties, the heyday of FSU football. In its 2012 class, FSU signed Mario Edwards of Denton, Texas, and Eddie Goldman of Washington, DC, ranked 1-2 among defensive tackles.

"That's what separates southern football from everywhere else in the country, defensive linemen," said Jimbo Fisher, the FSU coach.

Pugh is now a graduate assistant coach at Auburn. He will be good medicine for the young offensive linemen who sign with the Tigers in the next few seasons. He can warn them when they get a little lazy in practice. The baddest men on the planet are waiting on Saturday. There is no time to be lazy. Alabama's Johnson is trying to make his way in the NFL, but at least he had the training of the SEC to keep him competitive.

"You never got a week off against defensive linemen in the SEC," Johnson said. "Vanderbilt would give us a run for the money every year. People say they're not that good. They were good enough to make you play hard, let me tell you. You can't sleep on them. You can't sleep on anybody in the SEC."

CHAPTER 6

MUSCLE MATTERS

When Hugh Freeze sat before the Ole Miss committee picking the school's next football coach, Freeze was asked who his strength and conditioning coach would be.

"A Tommy Moffitt guy," Freeze said.

Which one, he was asked.

"Any of them," Freeze said.

Moffitt is the LSU strength and conditioning coach, and he has protégés just as Bill Parcells, Bill Walsh, or Tom Landry have protégés in the coaching ranks. The Tigers have won two national championships in football since Moffitt became their strength and conditioning coach (2003, 2007), and his influence is spread across weight-training rooms in the Southeast. One of his guys would be just fine with Freeze, and it didn't seem to matter which one.

Scott Cochran, the Alabama strength and conditioning coach, worked for Moffitt, and Cochran has been the strength coach for two national champions (2009, 2011) at Bama. After Ole Miss hired Freeze as its football coach in December 2011, Freeze hired Paul Jackson, who worked at LSU from 2007 to 2010 under Moffitt.

When Mickey Marotti, Florida's strength and conditioning coach for the Gators' 2006 and 2008 national champions, left Florida in December 2011 to rejoin Urban Meyer at Ohio State, the Gators hired Jeff Dillman, another "Moffitt guy," who worked at LSU in 2003, where he met the Gators' head coach, Will Muschamp. Muschamp called the hiring of the right strength and conditioning coach "critical" to the success he wanted to have at Florida.

Moffitt's way in the weight room is not the only way to a national championship, but his work is a useful illustration of what can go into a successful championship march. It is no longer enough to lift weights. There is a regimen to building players into what strength and conditioning coaches call "force producing machines." You can hear it throughout the programs in the conference: explode up through your ankles, through your knees, through your hips, and into the opposing player.

"Our goal is to put the strongest, fastest athlete on the field," Moffitt said.

Again, it is not just speed, which is what everyone thinks is the driving force behind the SEC. It is the strength that goes with speed. Muscle matters, and if you don't think so, consider the debate that went on before the final BCS poll in December 2011 that set the national championship matchup last January: LSU vs. Alabama.

Oklahoma State, a talented football team with one loss, could have been in the title game with its potent passing game (5,034 yards). Alabama, on the other hand, averaged 214 yards rushing per game, No. 16 in the nation. Oklahoma State was No. 58 rushing.

Alabama's rushing defense, where strength matters as much as speed, was No. 1. Oklahoma State was No. 90. At least one voter noticed the numbers and voted for inside-out football, that is, a game won by tackles, not receivers.

"I could have voted for either and slept well, but I voted for Alabama because they are more physical than Oklahoma State," said Gil Brandt, the former Cowboys executive who is a Harris poll voter. "The test was if the teams met on a neutral field, who would win? Alabama would win. I don't know that many people have physical players like Alabama and LSU."

Alabama slid into the National Championship Game ahead of Oklahoma State and won the title. Muscle played a part, plain and simple. It is more impressive when a team can run the ball and stop the run. Something about the ruggedness of the run demands respect. Mark Richt, the Georgia coach and a mastermind of offense, insists, "There is more than one way to skin a cat," which is true if you look at Oklahoma State's 12-1 record in 2011 and the Cowboys' highly skilled offense. But even with human pollsters bellyaching about the specter of an LSU-Alabama rematch, and the "boring" nature of LSU's regular-season win over the Crimson Tide, 9–6, muscle ruled the final vote. The voters sided with Alabama and they were not wrong.

"The SEC is a line-of-scrimmage league," said Marotti. "You have to have big, strong, tough offensive linemen and defensive linemen, or that speed we accumulated in cornerbacks and receivers is not going to work. We wanted to be the fastest team in the country, but we knew there was another part to the game."

The muscle is why coaches, such as Moffitt, matter in the SEC.

He is from Tennessee and attended Tennessee Tech, but Moffitt could not get a job at a high school in his home state after he finished college because football coaches said he would make their players too "muscle-bound." So in 1987 Moffitt hooked up with John Curtis, the football coach at the high school Curtis built called John Curtis, which he turned into a Louisiana football powerhouse.

Moffitt was turned loose by Curtis, who sent his young strength coach to seminars in New York, Dallas, and Atlanta, among other places. Moffitt wrote letters with questions to Johnny Parker, the strength coach of the New York Giants and confidant of Bill Parcells, and Parker would write back with answers to Moffitt's questions. Curtis allowed Moffitt to experiment with weight-training techniques as the pair tried to transform the football players at their small private school into "force producing machines."

The Curtis weight room had a disciplined atmosphere because Moffitt was the only coach and he did not want the players to get hurt experimenting on their own. He used video to study players' techniques, and Moffitt would draw stick figures on video screens to show a player's lean as he did weights. Was it the right technique? Was it teaching the proper mechanics in building that lean muscle? It wasn't about just lifting weights; it was being a technician and lifting weights to get the most out of the exercise.

"In J.T. [Curtis's] mind, nothing was ever good enough," Moffitt said. "I would come back to school with all this information, like what I learned from Coach [Gayle] Hatch in Baton Rouge, and all these other people, track coaches, you name it, and he would say, 'I like that, but what about this?' "

Moffitt reached down next to his desk and grabbed a thick binder full of yellowing paper. He plopped it down in front of him. It was all his notes and weight-lifting exercises from the nineties, and he still uses those exercises with the current LSU players. He started building the binder at Curtis and added to it in his jobs at Tennessee and the University of Miami.

"He [Curtis] got me to think outside the box before people were saying 'let's think outside the box,' " Moffitt said. "As strength and conditioning around the country went through these different phases of barbells and machines, and we all went through the phase of functional training for football, I stayed true to what I learned was effective."

There was an epiphany, the Aha! moment in weight training in the midnineties, that Moffitt points to as a major event in college football weight training. It didn't happen in the LSU weight room. It happened at Nebraska, which used to rule weight lifting in college football back in the 1970s and 1980s. The Cornhuskers' strength coaches did a study of players in the midnineties, and that study helped fuel Moffitt's drive for building a particular type of muscle.

"They found that the number one thing that correlated with a football player's success at the University of Nebraska was the amount of lean muscle they could put on the body of a football player," Moffitt said. "So what we have tried to do is choose the exercises where you are handling the most weight, and doing the most compound movements.

"You can do barbell movements here and only influence this small muscle here," Moffitt said, pointing to his chest.

"We chose exercises that required you to use lots of muscles. If you have a guy stand up and press large amounts of weight over their head, then you are influencing every muscle in your body. That's a jerk. I would prefer a 350-pound jerk over a 350-pound bench press any day. When you are using the bench press, you are using this small group of muscles here. When you are jerking the weight over your head, you are using every muscle group in your body. Football is not played one muscle group at a time. You are using your body as a unit when you play football."

There was no more sitting down on a Nautilus machine to lift. Playing football, who sits down? Moffitt wanted to build lean muscle throughout the body.

"We have a big variety of exercises. In a monthly training phase we're hitting twenty to twenty-five different exercises and offering a lot of variety and training heavy and hard and teaching proper lifting mechanics," Moffitt said. "When I worked for J.T., he insisted there were no boundaries. He wanted to be on the cutting edge, not just in lifting, but in running. People were still into long distances and having their players run miles and 800s and 400s.

"J.T. wanted me to do more explosive running. He wanted to get more done by doing less. Do as much as you can with the least amount of stress on the athlete. One reason for that is they were kids and their growth plates were not fully matured."

———

Moffitt does not want to spend time conditioning athletes when the LSU players start the summer off-season workouts. He wants them in condition when they show up so he can work on building force. So he tests them. On June 5, 2012, at 6:00 a.m. the LSU football players ran twenty-six 110-yard dashes. They did sixteen consecutive 110s, then took a five-minute break. Then they did ten more 110s to simulate overtime. If you passed the test, then the muscle-building could commence for the next six weeks.

Muscle is not easy to see from the couch, or from the press box, or from the seat three rows from the top of the upper deck. You have to watch the running back and see if he can get four yards, and do it again and again. You have to watch the SEC team that runs and runs and runs the ball and will not give up on the run just because there have been some 1-yard gains. SEC football is about driving the other guy backward and being able to win a football game from the inside out, tackle to tackle, on fourth-and-1 or fourth-and-goal when the contest is in the balance.

"There is always going to be a necessity to be sound from the center of the field out, always," said Les Miles, the LSU coach. "If you want to be able to run it, if you want to be able to throw it, you have to be sound from the inside out.

"All you have to do is give up an A gap and you will suddenly find out that throwing game you have designed and are ready to roll with ain't worth a damn. If you give up an A gap, there are not many runs you are going to enjoy, either."

Strength and conditioning coaches are vital to programs all across Division I football, but the SEC programs hunt these bodybuilders with the same fervor they hunt blue-chip defensive linemen. Moffitt has a formula for hiring his staff and he will not share it.

Only three coaches in an entire program of 125 players deal with every player while they are at a school: the head coach, the special-teams coach, and the strength and conditioning coach. When players report back in June for a six-week off-season program, no coaches are allowed to be with the team except the strength coach and his staff.

Moffitt is earnest in his work. Every day. He slides up to the edge of his seat behind his desk to make a point about leverage, the Holy Grail for football players. If you get underneath the pads of another football player, you can move that football player, even if you are forty to fifty pounds lighter. It is the foundation of SEC football. Muscle and leverage on top of speed. Moffitt rubs his hands together. This is what his job is all about, and he relishes teaching college players the fundamentals of strength.

"You can take a guy who is weaker and beat this guy all day long," Moffitt said after drawing one of his stick figures of a football player standing too erect. "We teach leverage. My guys who coach in this weight room are all former college football players. There are no exercise physiologists in here. We're not qualified to teach the zone play. We are highly qualified at teaching someone 'force production,' or applying force. That is basic. You have to be able to push."

He points to the smaller stick figure underneath a taller stick figure he has drawn in a notebook. "He's a force producing machine. He understands leverage. If you wait until August to teach leverage, you're in trouble. You hear coaches all the time say, 'he doesn't bend well.' You have to put him in positions to where he is producing force that is similar to football. We pick barbells off the ground and a lot of things where I am bending."

Moffitt slides the mouse for his computer and searches YouTube. He has an illustration to share about bending and force production and leverage. It involves Jacob Hester, a fullback, a short-yardage runner at just 200 pounds on the 2007 national championship team. Hester could get low and produce force, even against 260-pound linemen. Moffitt finds the YouTube clip he is looking for.

"Boom!" he shouts. It is Hester running through Major Wright, the all-SEC safety for Florida. A few players later, Hester is at the goal line bursting through heavier players for the winning touchdown against the Gators in a 2007 game.

"It gives me goose bumps," Moffitt says. "I'm not being ugly to Florida; this is just the way you do it."

The SEC takes this bending and quick "force production" seriously. When the University of Georgia was hunting for a defensive coordinator in December 2009, it circled around Kirby Smart, the defensive coordinator at Alabama. Mark Richt, the Georgia coach, wanted Smart, but he also had a notion to make it a package deal. Richt was considering going after the Tide's Cochran. Alabama, according to NFL scouts and some rivals, had gone to another level with its strength program under Cochran, right along with LSU.

You could see the difference just looking at the running back Trent Richardson. He is 5-foot-11, 224 pounds, and he was all shoulder pads and knee pads coming through the line. His arms bulged as he held the ball high and tight for security. The veins in his muscles popped through like a road map. His thick legs moved with force and resembled the quick chop of a sewing machine because he was so finely tuned by the Alabama strength and conditioning staff.

While Georgia pecked around Smart and Cochran, Nick Saban, the Alabama coach, was talking to Todd Grantham of the Cowboys, in case Smart left for Georgia. Smart stayed and Grantham took the Georgia job. Cochran stayed at Alabama, too. Smart got a raise for staying at Bama two years ago and another raise in April 2012 and currently makes $950,000 a year. Cochran got a raise to $325,000.

Georgia has overhauled its strength and conditioning program the last two seasons, especially after wilting in a number of games in the fourth quarter in 2010. Lack of depth had something to do with it, but Richt had to sacrifice somebody, and it was his longtime ally strength coach Dave Van Hallenger, who was the fitness guru to the national powerhouse teams at Florida State in the nineties.

Alabama has won two titles with the hyperactive Cochran in charge of weights. Auburn has a well-regarded strength coach in Kevin Yoxall, and the Tigers claimed the national title in 2010 with players swearing by the methods of "Yox," but Moffitt is still the kingpin of the SEC weight room.

When Miles took the job at LSU in January 2005, the first coach he talked to on Saban's staff was Moffitt. Miles already had the scouting report; he knew he wanted Moffitt to stay in Baton Rouge.

"Are you happy here?" Miles asked Moffitt.

Miles was relieved to hear a yes, and the partnership went from there. Miles is Moffitt's boss, but there is a two-way street of loyalty.

When Miles heard Moffitt's pay raise was trumped by Cochran's pay raise to $325,000, the LSU head coach shook his head from side to side with annoyance.

"You and me, we could sit down in a couple of hours and come up with a damn good weight-room regimen. I'm just telling you, we could," Miles said. "We would be pretty close to making these guys good. But if you ain't got a guy that can motivate your team when they walk into that weight room, it won't work."

That's why Meyer went back to Florida, a year after he left, and plucked Marotti, forty-seven, off the Gainesville campus and brought him to Ohio State. Meyer and Marotti were a relentless duo and would frequently talk about staying "in a player's jug" when it came to developing his body for the rigors of the SEC. They had one mandate for the Gators: be tough. Everything else came after being tough.

"We evaluated our program and how athletes were doing in our weight program based on toughness," Marotti said. "There are a lot of different methods out there, and they all work, but what we were doing was based on toughness through our mat drills, through some of our metabolic training programs, and a lot of mental-toughness things in the weight room."

Some days Marotti issued impossible challenges, something to prepare players for dealing with Alabama's Mark Ingram or LSU's Patrick Peterson, or some other SEC all-American. Marotti would back players into a corner by making them do lifts they had not attempted before. With Meyer's blessing, Marotti wanted to see who would fight back.

"The athletes fight or they don't," he said. "We put them in as many difficult situations as we could mentally so they learn to push through the breaking point. We had a lot of competition."

Florida used multiple disciplines of power lifting, Olympic lifting, and strength training. Obviously, Marotti focused on the things
that were going to help on the football field—hip strength, hip
power, explosiveness, speed—but everything always came back to
Meyer's favorite word, *toughness*. Marotti might order the players outside to do Strongman competitions such as tire flips and tug-of-war.
Tests of strength in sandpits provided excruciating resistance. All
you had to do to make Marotti angry was walk through the weight
room door not prepared to get better.

"If they came into the weight room with that bad demeanor and
low energy, they got sent out," he said. "That's how we did it. With
those Florida teams you saw the excitement in how they played because that's how they trained. The training intensity was second to
none. I would put it up with any program in the country. When you
have that intensity, you have that excitement, you have that fight-or-
flight syndrome.

"We had a saying at Florida: 'The tougher you are, the tougher
you get.' "

Marotti grew up in Ambridge, Pennsylvania, a steel mill town.
He lifted weights in the local VFW, and he knew tough. The Gators
came to learn tough and appreciate it.

Who can argue? The Gators won two national championships,
including one over Ohio State, Marotti's new employer. The Buckeyes should be willing to buy into Marotti's weight and conditioning
program because their predecessors got waxed by Florida's strength
and speed in the 2006 National Championship Game.

"The guys here always ask about those Florida kids, Tebow
and others," Marotti said. "How was this guy? How did they train?
They were very intrigued at what we did. We give some of the older

Ohio State players who come around some flak. 'It was kind of hard blocking those guys, wasn't it?' It's just different in the SEC."

How different? Jermaine Cunningham, a defensive end, arrived at Florida weighing 203 pounds. By the time he left, he was chasing quarterbacks at 255 pounds. All-SEC safety Ahmad Black was 163 pounds as a Florida freshman and left weighing 190. Halfback Chris Rainey was a mere 143 pounds when he entered Florida and left for the NFL in April 2012 a more fit 180 pounds.

"You have to look at genetic potential and forecast what they are going to look like in a year or two, but we had crazy changes. When these kids come in this light [weight], like Rainey, you go to the position coach and you say, 'Why in the world did you recruit this kid?' It was because of their athleticism. Strength is the easiest component to get better at. Speed is the one that is hard."

So Marotti and Moffitt and Cochran and Yoxall take the speed freaks and add muscle, which explains how SEC teams can deal with spread offenses when they have to. Football is not just about muscle up front, tackle to tackle. It is also about strength to latch on to a ball carrier or a receiver out in space where there is no help and get that offensive guy on the ground.

For instance, the Arkansas offense had its way with a lot of teams in the SEC in 2009, 2010, and 2011 and averaged 36 points a game in those three seasons. But against Alabama, with physical defensive backs, the Razorbacks' offense of isolating their receivers against single defensive backs did not produce the same yield. The Arkansas skill players were wrestled to the ground with force just after catching the ball and did not roll up many yards after catch. In the last three matchups with Alabama, Arkansas averaged 13 points a game.

"The size and strength of the corners is important," said Todd Grantham, the Georgia defensive coordinator, who worked for Alabama coach Nick Saban at Michigan State. "There is a misconception that you have to have fast people at corner, and it's true you have to have a certain amount of speed. But you need physical girth, too, because you have to tackle a wide receiver by yourself on those possession downs, those third-and-threes and third-and-fours. If you are not physical with them and too small, those big receivers are going to swat you."

One of the reasons Georgia had a downturn on defense after Brian VanGorder left as defensive coordinator in 2004 to join the Jacksonville Jaguars was that the Bulldogs were bringing in defensive backs who could not hold up. They were fast and could cover. But in the open field they needed help dragging down the bigger receivers.

"People thought Georgia had all this talent in their secondary because they were fast guys, but they were too small," said an NFL scout.

Look at the 2011 Georgia recruiting class. No defensive players taken were under six feet. Damian Swann, who was recruited by Alabama, is a 6-foot corner. Malcolm Mitchell, who was originally recruited as a corner, but switched to receiver in 2011, is 6-foot-1. Mitchell is expected to be back at cornerback for Georgia for the 2012 season.

"I talk to [Bill] Belichick and them now, and five-ten is the minimum they will take for a corner," Grantham said. "They won't take a corner under five-ten because of the possession routes and the heights of the receivers and things like that. The issue, when you get over a five-eleven for a corner, into the six-foot guys, is making sure the six-foot guy has the ability to transition, change direction, and have the movement skills to play man coverage on those tall wideouts. The five-elevenish guys are what you are looking for."

That's why Georgia was so disappointed it did not sign the 5-foot-11 high school cornerback Geno Smith, who played at St. Pius in Atlanta. He signed with Alabama in February 2012 and had all the skills the Crimson Tide—and the Bulldogs—wanted in a corner. He could tackle the tall receiver in space after a short pass and get them on the ground to stop that third-down possession and force a punt.

SEC schools, particularly the ones that have won a title in this golden era, have an edge with strength and conditioning. The weight coach can be a cult figure in the SEC, or at least a marketing star. Cochran has become so well-known at Alabama that a furniture dealer wanted him to be its pitchman, which would have been a lucrative deal if he had been able to accept it.

"As far as his [Cochran's] program, it's not that it is stuff you have never heard before," said Mike Johnson, a former Alabama offensive lineman who plays for the Atlanta Falcons. "What he does is push things beyond what you are used to. He doesn't like to do the same thing back to back. He makes sure you are getting heavy with all your lifts, so you will do cleans for a few weeks and go on to squats.

"He doesn't do anything halfway. They hand you a book at the start of each semester, each phase they call it, and it maps out where you are supposed to be going the next few weeks."

Johnson said the head coach at Alabama is busy recruiting in January and early February and cannot stand over his players in the weight room. It's why he has Cochran, a graduate of LSU and a native of New Orleans. Moffitt knew Cochran as a young boy and said the effervescent Cochran bounced around as a nine-year-old back home and has always been wound up around the game. He is particularly energized in the weight room to motivate Saban's players.

"That's one of his biggest assets," Johnson said. "He is Coach Saban's key to the team. He is how Coach Saban pushes his off-season on the team. Coach Saban does not come down to the weight room. He brought Cochran in for that Wednesday in February when football is just over and you are not looking forward to getting the next lift in.

"You might have just gotten done with a class or you have one to go to. Cochran's specialty is to make sure your mind is right. He gets loud."

Saban comes from the school that demands a big, physical football team. He was a thirty-nine-year-old assistant coach with the Cleveland Browns in 1991 when he worked with Bill Belichick, the head coach, and Michael Lombardi, who was Belichick's personnel man. They preached winning football from the inside out.

"That's why Bill and I got along so well. You have to be physically strong on the offensive and defensive line," said Lombardi, who works for NFL.com. "I believe that. Bill believes that. Nick Saban believes that. I believe the last position you should fix on your football team is wide receiver. You can't control the game from the outside in, you have to control it from the inside out. That's who we are."

Who they are at Alabama and LSU is muscle/explosion men. Moffitt and Cochran and other SEC strength coaches preach explosion. It is probably that way in other conferences, too, but considering the SEC's string of six straight national championships, they must be doing it better than other schools.

It is not Cochran et al. coaching by themselves in the weight room. There are plenty of assistant strength and conditioning coaches because the SEC makes a lot of money and can pay for extra help. Moffitt said the Big East, unable to keep up with the

SEC in strength and conditioning personnel, petitioned the NCAA to cut the number of allowable strength coaches. It was more than the Big East seeking relief. In an anonymous survey conducted by the Knight Commission, an overwhelming number of athletic directors and presidents said schools need to restrain themselves on the hiring of nonfootball assistant coaches because the costs are starting to get out of control. It was once reported that Alabama had twelve strength and conditioning coaches, but a rule being discussed will bring it down to no more than five strength coaches per program across all of college football.

The SEC is well stocked with weight coaches because it believes in muscle and running the football and has not been sucked into the outbreak of the spread offense around college football, with some exceptions. Florida proved a spread could work with Tim Tebow, and Auburn proved the spread could succeed with Cam Newton. The difference was Tebow and Newton brought a physical culture to the spread offense, which can be run-first and gap schemes, as opposed to pass-first and zone blocking on runs.

Newton and Tebow were powerfully built quarterbacks who made it difficult for defenses to police every gap because they played as two-way-skill players, a runner and a passer.

"When the quarterback's a runner, you create another blocker or a receiver that you have to cover," Nick Saban said. "So that kind of creates another gap on defense. And I think that's very difficult to defend."

Auburn tried to go to a spread under former head coach Tommy Tuberville in 2008, but that was a disaster with offensive coordinator Tony Franklin. The other Auburn coaches, so accustomed to I-formation football, did not buy into the system. Franklin was fired during the season, and Auburn ranked eighth in the SEC in total offense.

It is muscle, not formations and matchups on the perimeter, that wins football games. The rest of the conference has noticed. Before Georgia played LSU in the SEC Championship Game last December, the Bulldogs said they watched film of the Tigers' bullying of opponents with basic run plays, particularly a quick toss to one of their 225-pound running backs, who planted one foot and turned downhill to run.

"LSU and Alabama have pounded it into their heads that they are not going to let anybody be tougher," said Chris Burnette, Georgia's right guard. "If your mentality is nobody is going to whup you, a lot of times that's how it plays out. They know how to win with that style. Around here we're trying to get that culture going again."

Grantham, the Georgia defensive coordinator, noticed it, too.

"Your players have to understand that LSU physically attacked everybody they played," Grantham said in December 2011 before the SEC Championship Game. "They have really intimidated and bullied people. You have to understand what's going to happen when you play those guys. We're much more physical and more mentally tough than we were last year, or at the beginning of this season [2011]."

In general, college football has changed. It has become more perimeter-oriented, with fewer schemes that involve a fullback and a tight end. Many programs claim NFL scouts have put their most athletic players on offense. Quick passes to the wings are attempted to create mismatches, which means a talented third wide receiver matched up on a defense's fourth- or fifth-best defensive back.

"You can compete if you have great skill players, but at some point in time you are going to have make a fourth-and-one or stop somebody on fourth-and-one," said Phil Savage, the executive director of the Senior Bowl, former general manager of the Cleveland Browns, college scout and assistant coach. "That's where the rubber meets the road. That's one of the reasons the SEC has become a dominant conference. They are winning that battle up front. Generally, they have more depth and more players along the lines than other schools around the country."

No one has to ask NFL scouts what they prefer to see. They watch the spread offenses and the sliding, side-to-side blocking and derisively refer to it as "elephants left, elephants right." Alabama's Saban is a hero to scouts and trusted by them, not just because he feeds them lunch when they visit to watch film, but because he prefers to grind on opponents with the run game.

"As a scout you love to see physical run teams in a pro-style offense than the spread offense and dink and dunk," one scout said in a text message. The NFL has borrowed spread concepts and does some dinking and dunking of its own, but the best NFL teams, such as the Giants, are built to move down the middle of the field.

Before the 2009 LSU-Alabama game in Tuscaloosa, a group of NFL scouts squeezed onto the elevator at Alabama's Bryant-Denny Stadium. A scout from the Midwest was the last to get on the ride to the press box. He usually scouted teams from the Big 12 or Big Ten. He looked around at the other scouts on the elevator and said, "What is it with this league? Even the kickers are built up with some muscle."

The other scouts smiled. They understood.

There are no empty stomachs in the SEC.

"Why would I treat the kicker any different, he's a football player," Moffitt said. " 'Yeah, but he's a kicker,' they say. Well, he's our last line of defense. If something bad goes down, the kicker and punter are the last line of defense. Why would you want your kicker and punter to be some guy who has not picked up a barbell? He's going to get killed. If you run a fake kick and fake punt, the game is usually on the line. You get so much more confidence training with this stuff than sitting on the bench. He's not going to have much confidence having just stretched his hamstring all day or worked his hip flexor. Get him on the barbells.

"When we played Notre Dame in the Sugar Bowl, our kicker was Chris Jackson, and he ran a fake kick. He's on the ground. The guy from Notre Dame, the professional fighter [Tom Zbikowski], punched him. Knocked him out cold as a cucumber. Those kickers better be tough, too. The refs didn't see it. The game got dirty, dirty, dirty. Football is a tough game, and our kicker was right in the middle of it."

Moffitt flipped through his binder and stopped at a worn page, which was a definition of football given to him twenty years ago. He read it aloud:

" 'Football is a series of collisions with a test of strength, skill, and will. Big guys clearing the way for fast guys with countless contests of individual courage and toughness until one side collectively wears down physically or surrenders mentally.' "

Moffitt looked up and smiled. "Doesn't say anything about the spread offense, does it?"

CHAPTER 7

THE HANDOFF: ZOOK TO MEYER

It is nicknamed the Saban Rule, but if you witnessed the whirlwind recruiting tour of Ron Zook in the spring of 2002, where the Florida coach visited 101 high schools, you would know better. It is the Zook/Saban Rule. They both share in the NCAA's banishing of coaches from off-campus recruiting the four weeks after spring practice ends, usually April 1 to May 1, or April 15 to May 15. Many of their rivals wanted to play golf and relax; the frenetic duo of Zook and Saban wanted to hustle and work. The NCAA thought so much off-campus activity by head coaches was leading to violations of the "bump" rule, where coaches accidentally on purpose bump into a prospect and a casual greeting turns into a recruiting pitch, which is illegal that time of the year.

"I called him after they put that rule in; I knew who it was directed at," Zook said. "Guys like me and him and some other coaches. I was the first one I know of that went out all spring, and I know Nick worked extremely hard, too. We said to each other at the same time, 'How do we change this rule?' There are guys who didn't want to go out who had the power in the coaches convention to pass the rule. That's what happened. They put us on the sidelines."

Zook finished his declamation without taking a breath. That was him in the springtime; that was Zook all the time. Breathless. There was no time to breathe. For Zook, it was always the middle of the season, the middle of the fourth quarter. Rapid-fire Ron.

By the time the rule was changed in 2007 and April/May off-campus recruiting for head coaches was banned, it was too late for the rest of college football. Zook's 2002, 2003, and 2004 recruiting classes were the heart of the 2006 national champions at Florida under Urban Meyer. Twenty-two of the twenty-four players (kickers included) who started in the National Championship Game against Ohio State were Zook-recruited guys. Saban's 2003 recruiting class at LSU had key players in the Tigers' 2007 national title run under Les Miles. Zook was fired before the end of the 2004 season, and Saban left to coach the Miami Dolphins following LSU's 2004 season.

Besides working hard, Zook did something else radical for Florida, something that helped the Gators move forward. He ventured into the Bottom, what the Florida coaches called south Florida. He intruded on the University of Miami's turf with zeal and pirated away some players there, but he also beat the Hurricanes for other top high school talent elsewhere in the state. Miami's decline as a national power started for a few reasons, but one of them was the recruiting of Zook and his staff in 2002, 2003, and 2004, when they grabbed Florida players such as defensive tackle Ray McDonald of Pahokee, linebacker Earl Everett of Webster, Cornelius Ingram of Hawthorne, Andre Caldwell of Tampa, and Brandon Siler of Orlando, among others.

When the Hurricanes started to slide, it was one less national program to stop the surge of the SEC toward its six-year championship run. Florida State was already sliding with the loss of so many assistant coaches to head coaching jobs and the lack of a productive, consistent quarterback.

Zook's biggest recruiting success was Chris Leak, the quarterback from Charlotte, North Carolina. He was the centerpiece player of the 2003 recruiting class, not only because he was an accomplished quarterback, but because when he declared as a high school senior that he would play for the Gators, he did it on national television and urged Florida's other targeted recruits to follow him. Many did.

"That 2003 recruiting class is what got Florida back to that national championship expectation that they had in the nineties with Coach Spurrier," Leak said. "I was recruiting as much as Coach Zook was. Jarvis Moss was undecided and he was a Texas guy. I talked to him. Same with Andre Caldwell. He was undecided between Florida and Miami. We played together at the All-American Bowl. Andre was from Tampa and Miami was pulling hard to get him. He thought about committing there, but he became a Gator after we played the all-star game. Moss became a Gator, too.

"We had the best recruiting class in the country that year. It was a special class. LSU and SC were up there, but we had talent across the board. We came together for one purpose and that was to bring the Gators back."

It was a rough start for Leak at Florida because he felt he could play right away. His father, Curtis Leak, thought his son could play right away, too, and there were disagreements with Zook. Curtis Leak wanted his son to charge up the depth chart and take the reins in August practice, but Zook wouldn't let it happen too fast. He was not about to let his freshman get beat up too soon. But after four games of sharing the position in 2003, Leak's first year, there was no choice. Leak became the starter for the rest of the season and was named SEC Freshman of the Year.

"As players, you feel like you are ready to play right now. You have to have that drive," Chris Leak said. "I wanted that responsibility, the accountability. I wanted that weight on my shoulders and do what I came to do, which was to bring Florida back. I kept telling him, 'I'm ready to play, I'm ready to play.' He had a plan for me. He stuck to it and I had four great years at Florida."

Zook said he had to reassure Curtis Leak that his son would be groomed and taken care of. He told Leak, "Please, let us coach him. Trust us."

Leak left Florida the career leader in passing attempts (1,458) and completions (895). The majority of that was accomplished in two seasons under Urban Meyer (2005, 2006), but Leak gives a lot of credit to Zook for preparing him as a freshman and sophomore. He finished his career completing 61.4 percent of his passes and is the all-time Florida leader in passing yards (11,213).

More important, Florida was primed for a run at a national championship because Leak had been groomed, not rushed, and Zook had recruited plenty of stars to go with his quarterback. Zook's imprint on Goliath, this SEC run of championships, was in setting the table for Urban Meyer and the first title in the SEC six-pack.

The Gators were 9-4, 10-3, and 10-2 in Steve Spurrier's last three seasons in Gainesville (1999, 2000, 2001) before he departed for the Washington Redskins. In a competitive conference such as the SEC those were terrific records, but some holes needed to be filled. When athletic director Jeremy Foley filled the hole at the top with Zook to replace Spurrier, there was outrage. Mike Shanahan of the Denver Broncos and Bob Stoops of Oklahoma had turned down

Foley, and he turned to his friend who went by the nickname the Zooker.

Zook took over in 2002 and was 8-5, and a website was immediately revved up, Fireronzook.com. He was 8-5 again in 2003 and the noise and displeasure grew louder. His teams had a reputation for playing well in the first half of games, but not as well in the second half, and Zook was blamed for not making sufficient adjustments at halftime.

Lost in all the tumult was Zook's restocking Florida with players, enough players to win a national championship. The man could recruit. Could he ever.

Ron Zook's father was a traveling salesman and so was Ron Zook. He was a salesman for Florida football in the early nineties and then as head coach from 2002 to 2004. There was not a better recruiter in the SEC. Saban could haul in players, and so could Tennessee's Phillip Fulmer, but Zook was at least as good as they were. He and Saban ruled the conference in January and February of 2002 and 2003 by closing deals with high school talent.

Zook was relentless, which figures when you consider what he went through in Loudonville, Ohio, just to make the youth football team. His brother, Bob, would roll tires down a hill at Zook, who was just twelve. He had to stop the tires, then push them back up the hill as part of his training regimen. Zook's helmet, a basic white, had black tire marks on it from the collisions with the rubber, all of which had to be explained to Mrs. Zook when the boys walked in the door after a round of practice.

Some other quirks reveal Zook and the zeal with which he sold Florida and SEC football. He kept a tape recorder in his pocket and would snatch it out every so often during the day and make a quick comment to himself on something he did not want to forget. He would shave on the way to work in the morning, figuring the multitasking of driving and shaving could save a precious ten minutes.

Zook was always at work at 6:00 a.m., and to see him sprint from drill to drill during practice made it seem as if he were a freshman trying to impress the coaches with his hustle. "I try to give it all I got," he said. His father taught him the work ethic and would tell Zook often, "If you don't have time to do it right the first time, when are you going to have time to do it over?"

Does anybody outside of Florida remember Zook or credit his hustle for Florida's resurgence? They should. When national powerhouses Miami and Florida State started to show some cracks in 2003, Zook was right there chipping away at the Noles and Canes by picking up some of the best players in the state for the Gators.

He looked back at the Hurricanes' slide from prominence around 2003 and 2004, and said, "Maybe we had something to do with that."

Florida State started its slide because the terrific assistant coaches Bobby Bowden hired started to get their own head coaching jobs, such as Mark Richt, who went to Georgia, and Zook and his staff grabbed players that might have headed to FSU. Nick Saban's arrival at LSU hurt the Seminoles, too, and pushed them further from national championship contention.

"Zook doesn't get enough credit for what he did for the SEC back in 2002 and 2003," said recruiting analyst Tom Lemming. "The Big Ten, or ACC with Miami and Florida State, were always saying they were par with the SEC, but they weren't any longer when Zook got in full recruiting mode at Florida and Nick Saban arrived at LSU and then when Urban Meyer took over at Florida. Those three guys and Phil Fulmer did a lot for the SEC, in terms of recruiting and getting the SEC to where it is now."

Leak, twenty-six, called Zook "an unstoppable" force and still credits Zook for giving him a foundation for success.

"The thing that got me was how hard he worked," Leak said. "It wasn't a job to him because he loved what he did. He made me want to work harder. He set the pace for me. If you prepare as hard as he does, you have to win."

Not even his friends expected Zook to close all the ground he did with Miami. One of his friends, the former New Orleans head coach Jim Haslett, was watching the Hurricanes during a spring pro day for NFL scouts in 2002 and called Zook and said, "Man, you're in trouble. You have no chance against these guys."

Miami laid into the Gators in 2002, 41–16, which was Zook's first season.

"He was sort of kidding, but I knew what he was talking about," Zook said. "They had something like six players go in the first three rounds, and they were all from schools from West Palm Beach down.

"Coach Spurrier didn't like to go south, but I made up my mind we were going to stick our nose in down there. We called it the Bottom, and if we just got a couple of guys out of there, we would be okay. By that third year, we had gotten some players and might have had a little bit to do with Miami falling off a little bit. We got some of their guys."

Those guys included McDonald, a sensational defensive lineman from Pahokee.

"We went anywhere in Florida we wanted to go," Zook said. "We got into south Georgia and Atlanta, but you have to do a good job in the home state and the whole state, not just parts of it. When you go outside your state to recruit, the percentages go down."

Zook could not drive by car and recruit the way he wanted to; he had to fly. There were up-and-down trips all across the state in

2002 and 2003. He would visit high schools during the day and then speak to Gator clubs in the same town at night.

"Coach Spurrier would go on there and play golf during the day with the Gator club members and go to the meeting that night," Zook said. "When I went, I would jump on the plane, go to the schools during the day and then the meeting that night, and get back on the plane and go to the next place. During the day you were out selling the university, and at night you were out selling the university.

"There was no way I could cover as much ground as I did driving. I don't think I hit them all, but hit a bunch."

If a Gator club suddenly found itself on the list of dates to get a visit from the Florida head coach, it was not because Zook heard their chicken dinner was particularly good. He was giving lists to the athletic department of where the top recruits were and told them to schedule Gator club meetings in those towns. The pilot of the plane then got a list and away went the Zooker.

It unnerved other head coaches. Zook was too visible, too active. The season was a grind and some coaches wanted an end to it. They didn't want maniacs such as Zook and Saban on the recruiting trail and worrying whether they were getting an edge with casual contact with recruits. Zook and Saban treated recruiting like a hobby when other coaches treated it as a chore. The NCAA finally put in a rule that curtailed the head coaches' time on the road.

"What's the difference if I go out or not?" Zook said of his April/ May recruiting binges. "If you don't want to go out, don't go out."

Rival coaches started to accuse Zook of overpromising playing time to recruits. He was rolling, and the negative recruiting stories against Florida started to fly.

"We were not depleted, but we had some holes to fill. A lot of guys realized they would have an opportunity to come in and play early, possibly as freshmen," Zook said of his 2002 and 2003 classes. "We were accused of promising playing time; we never promised anybody they were going to play. We said you will have a chance to play early. Everybody jumped on board."

There was a difference between Spurrier and Zook. Spurrier will go down as one of the greatest coaches in college football history, and he understood he needed players, but he also thought he could take some players and coach them up. If he put them in the right scheme, they would succeed, even if they were less talented than the players across from them. Spurrier was that good of a ball coach, and his success at South Carolina proves it. He did not have better players than Alabama when he beat the Crimson Tide in 2010.

But Zook left nothing to chance when it came to talent. He went after the five-star player and wanted to overwhelm teams with pure skill.

"Having coached in the NFL, you learn how important talent is," Zook said. "You have got to have players. That's the one thing Coach Spurrier has grown to understand. You have to have players."

Indeed, Spurrier has realized in South Carolina that his dominant play-calling and schemes are not enough. The expectation with the Gamecocks was that his genius with the football would bridge the gap with the schools in talent-rich states such as Florida and Alabama and LSU. It has to some degree. The Gamecocks got in the SEC Championship Game for the first time under Spurrier in 2010. But there is still a talent gap.

"He's as good as there is coaching them up," Zook said, "but you have to get them."

Sometimes his assistants were better than Spurrier at spotting talent.

Late in the 1992 high school football season, Spurrier, Zook, who was an assistant, and Bobby Sanders, another assistant coach, went to watch Fort Walton Beach play in the state championship and get another look at a high school senior, Danny Wuerffel. Spurrier, Zook said, was not sold on Wuerffel because of his throwing motion. Sanders had been recruiting Wuerffel and pleading with Spurrier to sign the son of a military preacher, who was leaning toward Florida State and getting a late recruiting push from Alabama.

The night the Florida coaches went to watch Fort Walton play, Wuerffel dominated the play-off game and his team won. Spurrier looked at Sanders and said, "Bobby, maybe we should really get this Danny Wuerffel kid."

On the ensuing recruiting visit to Wuerffel's house, Zook slapped Wuerffel on the arm on the way out the door and said, "Danny, the last Heisman Trophy winner at Florida was a quarterback, who was the son of preacher. Be a Gator and make it two."

Wuerffel signed with the Gators and won the Heisman and led the Gators to the 1996 national championship. The next Florida quarterback to win the Heisman was also the son of a preacher man: Tim Tebow. That's three preacher's sons with Heisman hardware.

Zook knew how to make a pitch, and sometimes he even got help from his family, sort of.

"We were recruiting Juice Williams for Illinois, a highly rated quarterback, and he was at the house for dinner with the parents for an official visit," Zook said. "My youngest daughter was helping serve about the time I told Juice's mother, 'I am going to treat Juice just like my own children.'

"My daughter leaned over and said, 'He may not like that.'" Williams signed with Illinois anyway.

Zook's success in recruiting never translated to the field, at least while he was at Florida. Zook's best recruiting class (2003) was made up of sophomores in 2004, but athletic director Jeremy Foley had seen enough. The Gators were on their way to a 7-5 season in 2004. There was a last-second loss to Tennessee, 30–28, but the clincher was probably a 38–31 loss at Mississippi State.

Zook knew he was out even before the October 30 loss to Georgia. But he refused to walk away. Foley asked him to stay, and Zook obliged through the end of the regular season. Some coaches, perhaps being made bitter by the firing, would have ripped the door off the hinges on their way out and left the players to the rest of the staff. Not Zook. "When they fired him before the 2004 season was over, him staying with the team after that happened showed how much he cared about that team," Leak said. "He didn't have to stay. He could have gone on his way. He was committed to us."

Foley fired Zook before the season was over because the athletic director was always thinking ahead, always a step in front of others for the good of Florida. It gave him an extra month to search for a coach. He didn't have to lie to people about Zook and his future and let Zook twist in the wind. If Foley got out there searching for a new coach, someone would find out, and there would be backbiting that Florida was not loyal and was undermining its own coach.

But who could Foley find that could recruit like Zook and then coach the five-star recruit? Who was that charged up and fanatical?

Urban Meyer, that's who.

He had the zeal of Zook. If you wanted to, you could make it a three-headed name on that rule barring head coaches from the recruiting road in the spring: Zook/Saban/Meyer. Like Zook, Meyer was from Ohio and he always brought his fastball when he was recruiting.

Meyer, who left Florida following the 2010 season, was playing in the Chick-fil-A Charity Golf Classic at Reynolds Plantation after Ohio State's spring practice in 2012 because of that rule that keeps head coaches off the recruiting trail in the spring. "Every day I was out there on the road," Meyer said of spring recruiting, "I think most of the guys went out. I went out. I can't go out now. That's why I'm here playing golf."

Meyer was the coach at Utah, and the Utes were finishing up a 12-0 season when Foley set his sights on him. Notre Dame was also interested, but it wasn't a fair fight. Florida had more money, and it had what every coach covets: access to fertile recruiting ground.

"It was close, real close," Meyer said of the Notre Dame versus Florida sweepstakes. "The recruiting area was the best; the athletic director at Florida was great.

"The kids and my wife wanted to go to Florida."

Meyer's first class at Florida in 2005, which was eighteen players, was ranked fifteenth nationally, but that included safety Reggie Nelson, who was originally signed by Zook but could not qualify and had to go to junior college. But when Meyer had his feet on the ground and had it all mapped out and had his wardrobe all orange and blue, he was a master in hauling in prospects. His next recruiting season, the 2006 class, included Tim Tebow and Percy Harvin, who were significant contributors to the 2006 championship team as freshmen.

But before there was Meyer and Tebow, there was Meyer and Leak. It was supposed to be an ill-fitting partnership. Meyer had brought his spread scheme from Utah, which featured some runs by the quarterback on the option. Leak was more of a classic quarterback, a vertical-route thrower who needed play-action passes and a fullback to keep the defense from being too freewheeling on the rush.

Sure enough, Meyer and Leak were tethered by a thin string. It didn't look promising, especially with that visit to Alabama on October 1, 2005.

Meyer remembers walking out onto the turf of Bryant-Denny Stadium and the scoreboard growling at him with this scratchy, omnipresent voice. The voice of Bear Bryant. The stadium was already in a frenzy when Himself could be heard over the stadium sound system with that deep, bass voice extolling the virtues of the Crimson Tide.

"I was thinking, Man, you're in the big city now. Bear Bryant's talking to you from the scoreboard," Meyer said. "You know it's prime time."

Life in the big city was wretched that afternoon. Leak was sacked four times. His streak of 118 passes without an interception was stopped 3 shy of Wuerffel's school record. His receivers were spread out, as usual, but Alabama came after him with fury and did not give him time to find the open man. The Gators were crushed, 31–3.

The loss to Alabama was Urban Meyer's first loss since the 2003 season at Utah, a streak of twenty straight wins. It was the first time in his head coaching career his team had not scored a touchdown. Underneath the grandstands after the game, Meyer left the Florida locker room alone. He stopped for a moment and put his head down in the dim light. Several years later he admitted to rethinking his marriage to the spread in a conference that was so ferocious with defensive linemen who could rush.

"I was very concerned," Meyer said.

It got better in two weeks, but not by much. Florida lost to LSU, 21–17, on October 15. Leak was sacked four times again and was 11 for 30 passing. The Gators were 5-2. The quarterback, now a junior, understood the issues in protection and coverages with the spread; it was just a matter of talking to Meyer about making some adjustments.

"We were five-wide and teams knew what we were going to do by what formations," Leak said. "I was getting hit, which is fine. I could take it, but it was hurting the offense."

Georgia was next, and Leak wanted to go to Meyer with suggestions, but not demands. But the rest of the state of Florida had the demands on Meyer. He was ridiculed for thinking he could bring what the critics called a school yard, 7-on-7 offense into the SEC. His spread looked overmatched by the size and speed of SEC defenses, and maybe, just maybe, he was not the best man for the job of bringing the Gators back to glory.

But Meyer was the guy. His offense needed some tinkering, and the protection for the quarterback would be provided in time. What Meyer did first was keep the program united. He did that by not ridiculing anything Zook and his staff did, or didn't do. The players were Meyer's guys now, but he knew they liked Zook, the coach who'd recruited them. When Meyer and his staff got together for the first time in the Florida football offices the winter of 2005, he looked at his assistant coaches and told them, "Any one of you says a negative thing about the staff that just left and I hear it, I'll fire you. I mean it. They don't deserve it."

Several months later, in early February, Meyer gathered the staff and their wives and children and the players in a meeting room at the stadium at ten o'clock at night. Some troublemakers were in the program, and Meyer pointed to the coaches and their families and told the players, "You're not going to ruin things for these families." He told the players there would be suspensions. The delinquent behavior off the field had to stop.

Meyer had Charlie Strong, the defensive coordinator and a hold-over from Zook's staff, speak to the team. "That was big," said Leak. Some players spoke, too. The Zook guys, some still bitter over his firing, were coming together with Meyer and his staff.

"We had to take a leap of faith," Leak said. "They didn't know us, we didn't know them. I spoke. Charlie Strong spoke. That meeting was a big step in the right direction. Until you make that leap of faith, things might not work well; usually, you have to go through adversity. The meeting was nine o'clock, ten o'clock at night. Everyone was called in. Charlie Strong was a big factor; everybody respected Charlie Strong." Later in the Meyer tenure, Meyer had a rash of discipline problems, but in 2005 and 2006 things settled down and it was football.

So the last week in October 2005, with some trust built up, Leak thought he could be frank with his head coach, whom he had known less than a year. It was late Monday morning with the Georgia game in five days.

"I went to Coach Meyer to ask him about having a lot more flexibility at the line of scrimmage with play-calling," Leak said. "I took him some plays that the whole offense liked and we had success at.

"You know what he said? 'Fine, I love it. Let's go.' "

Urban Meyer's reputation was as an offensive guru, a tactician who could draw up a play in the dirt on the sideline and have it work. He was the master at putting defensive backs on an island in matchups he wanted and letting receivers win the game in space. He could get two blockers on one defender by design and teach the quarterback how to make the right read on the option. This was a coach who was going to win two national championships and do it from inside the SEC. Meyer, with a résumé full of credentials, sat and listened to a twenty-year-old kid talk to him about what worked and what didn't work on offense.

"Chris Leak earned that right," Meyer said. "Chris Leak was one of the hardest-working guys in our program. He was completely invested in our program. He never gets enough credit. We were planning on doing some things anyway, but to hear your quarterback want to take ownership of the team and what we were doing, that was great. To this day, if someone wants to take ownership and they have earned it, they are going to get it."

One of the adjustments was to make sure Leak had some protection in the backfield. The walk-on fullback Billy Latsko became key; so did the 220-pound running back DeShawn Wynn.

"We were able to transition to a power running game when we had to," Leak said. "That was big, especially in the SEC. You had to keep those defenses honest. Billy was a Gator great. His ability to catch the ball out of the backfield and his ability to block were big. He was the unsung hero.

"Coach Meyer's offense at Utah did not use a fullback at all. That was one of the things we transitioned into. Coach Meyer realized you had to have some kind of power run game. That power run game gave us that toughness, that attitude factor. You need that in the SEC."

The meeting of the minds came just in time to avoid a loss to the bitter rival Georgia.

The fourth-ranked Bulldogs were good again on defense in 2005, they were 7-0, and there was a buzz in Athens that the season could be shaping up as a run to the national championship. It was a transition season at quarterback with Joe Tereshinski III, but the defense was heavy-handed and could win games by itself.

The first time Florida touched the ball, it went 80 yards in thirteen plays. Seven of the plays were runs. Leak capped the drive with a 3-yard run for a touchdown. The Gators won the game, 14–10. Meyer could take off his flak jacket.

Florida finished 9-3 in 2005 in Meyer's first season, a good record considering all the injuries. Prized receiver Andre Caldwell broke his leg in the third game. Tight end Jemalle Cornelius suffered a stress fracture in an ankle. Receiver Dallas Baker had a broken rib, which led to a punctured lung. Vernell Brown broke his leg.

What was really significant was the foundation that was poured. The Gators had a power element to go with a productive passer, and not only was Leak coming back in 2006, the defense would be fully mature with untamable defensive linemen who would assault quarterbacks throughout the drive to the national championship. Meyer then added a couple of key pieces—Tebow and Harvin—and the Gators were setting themselves up for a title run.

"My emotion when I came here was to win Florida a national championship regardless of what we had to go through," Leak said. "We were on a mission to get Florida back to the national championship. We were all committed to that."

Meyer was committed to that, as well, so in the spring of 2006 he went to Los Angeles to trade notes with Southern California coach Pete Carroll, who is regarded as a defensive mastermind. But something else caught Meyer's eye in L.A. He looked around at the Trojans' facilities and there was no *Wow!* factor. There were *just* trophies, no glitz, and no glamour, even for a school in ritzy L.A. There were no wide-screen televisions or joysticks connected to video-game boards trumpeting the Trojans' success. The facilities were average, even though the tradition and accomplishments were anything but average.

When Meyer returned to campus at Gainesville, he walked into a meeting with athletic director Jeremy Foley and associate athletic director Greg McGarity and said, "I have nothing to complain about."

Florida, even with the 1996 national championship and the six SEC championships it won under Steve Spurrier, had not entered the *Wow!* arms race with facilities. Its trophies were on display in a modest reception area leading toward Meyer's office, with no extra touches of flat screens and archways and towering glass windows and display cases and expansive foyers to entertain recruits and their parents. There wasn't much curb appeal.

You walked up a stairway to the Gators' football offices and it seemed like just another football office, not home to one of the most preeminent college football programs in America. Nothing showed off the rich history of the program. There was no polished weight room. No *Wow!* Meyer considered what he had seen at Southern Cal, but he was not in the Pac-10. This was the ferocious SEC, the kings of recruiting lived in this conference. Meyer knew the Gators had to jump back into the arms race with a posh football facility. There had to be an upgrade and Foley knew it, too.

"You either get better or get worse, you never stay the same," Meyer said. "It had to happen. We needed that front door for the program to showcase what Florida football was about. You fall behind if you don't try to keep moving forward."

Meyer understood in 2006 that the college game was entering an era of splash where recruits had to see the *Wow!* It was just the way it was. The generation of recruits who had grown up with video-on-demand and flat-screen TVs was going to be influenced, to a degree, by glitz.

"We were putting down the new carpet, painting what we had to paint every year, keeping it clean, and we were winning," said McGarity, who is now the athletic director at Georgia. "We improved the locker room for the student-athletes and expanded the stadium. It was not the NFL, but we had met the requirements for college football. What we didn't have in facilities did not prevent Steve Spurrier from winning in the nineties.

"But what you have to do is take away the negatives. We kept working on taking away the negatives."

Florida had already taken away some negatives and pushed into the plush. Before the 2003 season, construction was completed on a $50 million expansion/renovation of the west end of Ben Hill Griffin Stadium, otherwise known as the Swamp. Twenty-nine hundred luxury club seats were installed, and thirty-four private suites were funded by boosters.

More was to come because Foley understood where the game was going and the impact of a grand ballroom, so to speak, to highlight the accomplishments of the football program. On their way to lunch one day, Foley stopped McGarity and pointed to this "hole" in the southwest corner of Ben Hill Griffin Stadium—a grass embankment kept in place by a concrete wall.

"What about that?" Foley said, pointing to the open space between sideline stands and end-zone stands, outside the concrete concourse.

The open space could be connected to the Swamp. It could be Florida's grand ballroom, a showpiece to go with the stadium's renovations, which included the press box and skyboxes for boosters and guests. This could be the front porch that would hold the national championship trophies and SEC trophies and the Heisman replicas.

When recruits walked into the facility, they would be impressed. Did recruits and their parents really understand how successful the Gators had been? Maybe, but just to make sure, there would be this exclamation point, a showroom of Florida football.

The recruits and their families would have no choice but to go *"Wow!"* It was the art of the deal.

James W. "Bill" Heavener, the college roommate of Bob Tebow, the father of Tim Tebow, planted the first stake in the ground with an $8 million donation. The spigot opened and sixteen donors contributed $28 million to the project. The project was 100 percent privately funded and opened in August 2008. Florida football was on its way, and many considered it the top program in the country with a coach, talent, and facilities to match. The Gators won another national championship in 2008, and, indeed, no other program was on the same pedestal as Florida.

Ron Zook helped get the Gators there.

On January 8, 2007, Zook was sitting in his hotel room at the coaches' convention in San Antonio with his wife, Denise, watching Florida play Ohio State for the national championship. He was the head coach at Illinois now and he was from Ohio, but its being Ohio State, a Big Ten team, did not matter at all to Zook.

"I was pulling hard for Florida. Even though I was from Ohio and I like Ohio State, I wanted the Gators to win," Zook said. "I suppose I could have been bitter, but it's about the kids. It's about them accomplishing what I said we were going to do, what they said they were going to do. I couldn't be there, but I felt like I had a little something to do with it."

His players didn't forget. In the euphoria of the locker room after the game, they brought up Zook's name; he started it all, they thought, and he must be proud of them. They knew where credit should go. Meyer was their coach, but so was Zook. It was a matter of loyalty.

"I called Coach Zook. It wasn't that night; it was crazy that night after the game. But I got him the next morning, early," Leak said. "I told him he was just as much a part of it as I was. Twenty-two of those seniors were his guys, guys recruited by Ron Zook. Let me tell you, we felt his presence.

"It's the truth. We were Ron Zook's guys. The credit was earned by him, not given. You know, I talked to Coach Zook a couple of weeks ago. What is it—ten years after he recruited me?—and I still talk to him. The relationship goes beyond football with some coaches."

CHAPTER 8

GOOD AND LUCKY
2006 Gators, 2007 Tigers

Messengers kept coming down the aisle every few minutes. "Pitt's winning."

They walked back and forth a couple more times on the flight back to Baton Rouge, from the front of the plane to the back of the plane, giving the partial score of the West Virginia–Pitt game. It was too tedious for Les Miles and he finally had enough.

"I'm not the guy who wants to get a partial score," the LSU coach said. "You're not going to break my heart with scores here and there. You better give it to me at the end. I'm not going to sit there saying, 'Oh, oh, oh, jeez. You better come up with a final score for me.'

"I said, 'Okay, guys, I'm done with that s***.' You tell me when the game is over."

Miles was seated in the middle of the plane. His seniors are always up in first class, closest to the cockpit, which was getting the news from the ground, and that was just fine with the LSU coach. He didn't want to be on the edge of his seat. He wanted to lean back in his seat and revel in what was already accomplished: an SEC championship won that night over Tennessee. It was December 1, 2007.

"Playing for a conference championship is awfully damn important here," Miles said. "Even this past season [2011] we're going to hang two banners in this building. A Western Division banner and the SEC banner. Those are damn important things and they were damn important in 2007."

West Virginia could wait . . . for another hour. Miles surely wanted to play for a national championship, but he had his hands around the SEC championship trophy. That was enough for the time being. Others had to get out of the way of his joy.

When the plane landed, Miles heard the final score: Pitt 13, No. 2 West Virginia 9. It had all been lined up for the Tigers; LSU had a chance to play for the national championship. West Virginia had been a decisive favorite against the Panthers, who were just 4-7, but the Mountaineers unraveled. Their sensational quarterback, Pat White, dislocated his thumb in the second quarter, the Mountaineers lost three fumbles, and WVU became the sixth team ranked No. 2 in 2007 to lose. Pretty lucky, huh? For LSU, that is.

Miles, sitting in his office in Baton Rouge four and a half years later, just smiled. Pat McAfee, an NFL-caliber kicker, second-team All Big East, had missed two makeable field goals for West Virginia. How could that happen? Miles turned his right hand over, the palm was up, and he kept smiling and gave a little shrug. A Bible was a few feet away on his coffee table. You knew what he meant. A blessing had flowed into his open palm. He believed that.

"We got on the plane having won the conference championship," Miles said. "We got off the plane with a chance to win the national championship. Are you kidding me? How wonderful all that was."

It was not so wonderful for West Virginia. After this bitter loss on a bitter-cold night, plenty of ill will followed. Some students gathered outside McAfee's off-campus apartment and started shouting threats and honking horns. Texts warned of abuse for missing field goals from 20 and 32 yards. His car was vandalized and then there was the ultimate smack talk: a death threat.

"It was just a nightmare," West Virginia coach Rich Rodriguez said after the game. "The whole thing was a nightmare."

For LSU, it was euphoria. Just to make sure the BCS did not dare slip anyone but LSU into the National Championship Game against Ohio State, Miles was given directives on the tarmac on whom to lobby in the media to make it all secure. Les the Lobbyist got on ESPN and started talking up the Tigers. Undefeated in regulation, he chimed, a phrase coined by his wife, Kathy. LSU (10-2) had lost to Kentucky and to Arkansas, both in triple overtime. They had clobbered No. 9 Virginia Tech and beat Tim Tebow and No. 5 Florida. They won at No. 18 Tennessee and beat Nick Saban's first Alabama team in Tuscaloosa.

"Georgia wanted to say it was the hotter team and it should play Ohio State," Miles said. "Well, I said the hell with them. We were the better team. They didn't even win their side of the conference.

"We had accomplished greatly, even if we didn't get in that last game. It didn't make any stinking difference where we played after we won the championship of this conference. But I'm glad we got the shot. It was going to give us a chance to get healthy. Glenn [Dorsey] needed the time off, and Matt Flynn didn't even play in the conference championship game. When we got healthy, well, you saw it."

The Tigers waxed the Buckeyes. They were good and lucky.

They were more than that, though. They were a together team. Some significant players on the '07 championship team, such as Dorsey, the all-American defensive tackle, were recruited by Saban, who had left for the Miami Dolphins following the 2004 season.

Then the Miles recruits were mixed in with the players left behind by Saban. A visitor to Miles's office wanted to talk about Saban's guys, but Miles held his hand up as a stop sign.

"No, no," said Miles. "When I got here, they became my guys. They were my guys."

The players, meanwhile, treated it as if they belonged to neither Saban nor Miles. They were LSU guys. That's how LSU has remained near the top of the heap in college football the last five seasons: Louisiana pride. People around the state recognize that high school players, staying in state, can deliver championship after championship.

"Eighty percent of the guys in the program were from Louisiana," said Craig Steltz, the safety for the 2007 team. "It doesn't matter for a lot of guys who the coach is, Saban or Miles. We are going to uphold the traditions of the program. We are going to wear the white jerseys and gold pants at home. We're going to run through the goalposts and walk down the [Victory] hill. The tradition is what has to be upheld through the years."

That was fine by Miles. Players first, coach second. Miles made the mistake one time of getting the order wrong. It still bugs him. He remembers referring to his guys after one game while he was the head coach at Oklahoma State as "they," and he has never forgotten it. "We were at Kansas State and we got the s*** kicked out of us," he said. "We had suspended two fullbacks and had some injuries and it was just a bad day, and I, as a young head coach, put myself in a separate place and said 'they' when responding to a question. I had to apologize to my team. It so bothered me."

So Miles will not enlighten the media, and by extension the public, after a bad play, or a bad loss, if it means heaping some shame on one of his players. A lot of coaches are like that, but Miles is really like that, and it's how that 2007 season happened the way it did with harmony and goodwill and no finger-pointing after two crushing triple-overtime losses.

"Here's the fundamental with me. My opinion counts, and fundamentally they [reporters] need enlightenment with my team from me," he said. "Their opinion does not count. I understand people from the outside looking in and their helplessness. I am trying to help as much as I can. But let me tell you what happens and why you don't get enlightened all the time. We're playing Tennessee in the SEC Championship Game (2007). Matt Flynn is my holder; he's out, injured. Ryan Perrilloux is my new holder. There is just a little difference in how it all needs to mesh on the kick. Those things you as a reporter are never going to get from me."

Colt David missed a 30-yard field goal before the half in the 21–14 win over the Vols. David did not miss many 30-yard field goals in his career, but he had an alibi, a new holder. Miles refused to lay blame or enlighten.

It's why Miles did not jump down Bobby Hebert's throat publicly in the press conference following the 21–0 loss to Alabama in the national championship in January 2012. Hebert, a former NFL quarterback, popular radio talk-show host in New Orleans, and father of one of Miles's players, asked an agitated question about why Miles did not change quarterbacks against Alabama with the offense flailing away. The answer was pretty obvious: Jarrett Lee, whom Hebert wanted in the game, had wilted in Tuscaloosa in the 9–6 LSU win in November when Lee had to pass against Bama pressure. Miles wouldn't say publicly that Lee was not going to handle the frothed-up Alabama defense any better in the rematch. Others knew it, but we don't know what Miles believed because he kept his mouth shut on his quarterbacks.

"You're never going to get the comparisons from me for Jordan

Jefferson and Jarrett Lee in that championship game," Miles said. "I am going to stand for both of them. I love both of them."

Even after Jefferson went on an Atlanta radio station a month after the game and bashed the LSU game plan against Alabama, Miles kept quiet. Others in the program were incredulous at Jefferson's sniping. Miles had stood behind Jefferson after the quarterback was in a bar fight before the 2011 season and stuck with Jefferson as quarterback after a number of poor passing performances. It wasn't just the game plan that cost LSU against Alabama; it was Jefferson's mishandling snaps from center and penalties that ruined some plays. Miles needed a flak jacket with his own side taking shots at him, but he was mum.

And that is the essence of Les Miles. His record is 75-18 at LSU, an .806 winning percentage.

He is considered a players' coach, but he does not coddle players. He tells them rather directly, "When you sign up to come to this school, you are signing up to really exceed expectations." Miles can do nothing about the expectations of fans and tells his players they will have to deal with it and tighten their seat belts and get ready for it. It was that way at Florida when the wheels came off during Urban Meyer's last season and criticism mounted of a coach who had won two national championships. It has been that way at Georgia the last four years. Auburn players needed layers of thick skin in the 2011 season, just one year after winning a title. Honeymoons are extra short in the SEC.

Yeah, but what's Miles good at besides defending his players and inspiring them before games? You know, the Xs and Os stuff? What does he know? We know Saban knows defense and Urban Meyer knows offense and Gene Chizik knows defense. We read this tripe that Miles is good at "organization" and stuff like that. Well, here's what Miles knows. The SEC is a line-of-scrimmage league, and Miles, an offensive lineman for Michigan in the seventies, understands line play on both sides of the ball, and if you look at his teams, they resemble Goliath in every way. Yes, there is plenty of speed, but the Tigers have big backs and stout lines on both sides of the ball in most seasons. That's what Les Miles knows. How to shove the ball down your throat the way Woody and Bo taught him when he played and coached in the Big Ten.

Here's what else Miles knows. How to rebound. The Tigers, Steltz said, never had back–to-back losses in Miles's first three years. Only once in six seasons has LSU had back-to-back losses under Miles.

Not everyone likes Miles. He seems to have trouble with guys named Bob. First Hebert, then Petrino.

When Miles sent his field-goal kicker out at Tiger Stadium against Arkansas in 2011 to make a 38–17 lead a 41–17 lead, Bobby Petrino, the Razorbacks' coach, shook his finger toward Miles and yelled, "[Expletives]!"

Of course, we can always tie Les Miles's identity and his strengths as a coach right back to some intangible, such as poise for not throwing his postgame microphone at Hebert and shouting right back at this parent of one of his players. Miles could have looked stunned and hurt because when the LSU fans had climbed all over Miles in past seasons, Hebert had defended Miles. The LSU coach listened to the Hebert rant, which was posed as a question, for forty-five seconds and was unmoved. A day later, Hebert ripped Miles again, with the former quarterback going on a national radio show and claiming he had forgotten more football than Les Miles knew.

Four months later, Miles smiles. He does not have to rejoin this parent-coach skirmish if he doesn't want to and he doesn't want to.

But why didn't he come unglued with Hebert lashing him? It's the same reason Miles is not a raving lunatic on the sidelines when coverage is blown or a block is missed.

"My team sees and recognizes poise. If they don't see it and recognize it, then they don't display it," Miles said. "That's when you have an opportunity for some real bad examples to be set on the field.

> *As a coach, it does not do my team any good to make determinations about who is at fault and me having the personal liberty to lose my focus on what's going to make us a better team. Poise is fundamental to the head coaching position if you want to win the game.*
>
> *I'm much more discriminating in practice. If we need to get something fixed, we need to get it fixed right there. Adjustments need to be made in games, sure, but when you get to the game as players and you have busted your tail and done everything you have been asked to do, heaven forbid the coach who takes the liberty to go off for something, frankly, the coach allowed to happen with poor preparation.*

And that again is the essence of Les Miles, a good and lucky coach in 2007.

And then there was the good and lucky team from Florida, the 2006 Gators. They had a door open, magically, by the same 13–9 score that would open the door for LSU a year later.

In 2006, while Florida was playing Arkansas for the SEC championship in the Georgia Dome, No. 2 Southern California lost to 6-5 UCLA, 13–9. It was the SEC's big dose of luck to go with a big dose of talent. The Trojans had pummeled the Bruins, 66–19, in 2005, and they thought they were going to do it again in 2006, but they couldn't handle UCLA's pressure defense.

So the day UCLA stunned USC, No. 4 Florida slipped into the 2006 National Championship Game against Ohio State with a 38–28 win over Arkansas. It was an odd scene in the Georgia Dome at halftime of the Florida-Arkansas game. While the bands were performing on the field, the Gators fans were crammed into concourses watching televisions and roaring with each UCLA big play on defense against Southern Cal. When the West Coast upset was complete, a reporter hustled down to the locker rooms on the ground floor of the Georgia Dome. A Florida team manager was stopped on his way back to the field for the second half and asked, "Do the players know about USC losing?"

"They know," said the manager.

They didn't know. A handful of student managers, and a couple of players, knew, but most of the Gators did not know. They had other things to worry about. They led the Razorbacks by just 17–7 at the half, and their quarterback, Chris Leak, was in no shape to play the second half. He had sprained his right throwing hand and couldn't grip the ball without considerable pain.

"They numbed my hand at halftime," Leak said, "but then I couldn't feel the ball in my hand, and I was wondering how I was going to get some touch and some feel on my throws. It's one of those things you hope you never have to go through, especially in a situation like that."

Leak thought about wearing a glove, but what good would that do if he couldn't feel the football? Things did not start well for the Gators in the third quarter. The Razorbacks scored 14 points to take a 21–17 lead. Florida tried to get Percy Harvin, their wondrous freshman hybrid back/receiver, involved in the offense as much as they could to take the pressure off Leak, so they tried a shovel pass into the middle of the line. It was intercepted and returned for a touchdown.

Finally, in the fourth quarter, Leak started to get some feeling back in his hand. The Gators led 31–28 when they went on an 80-yard drive for a touchdown. Leak completed 3 of 4 passes for 57 yards, and Florida led 38–28. The Gators defense continued to limit the Razorbacks' terrific halfback Darren McFadden (21 carries, 73 yards), and they finished off Arkansas for the win and the SEC championship. Then the Gators—all of them—found out USC had lost and they had a chance to play for the title.

So there was still one more game Leak and the seniors needed to win to complete what they'd started under former coach Ron Zook. The Gators faced Ohio State in the National Championship Game and put away the unbeaten Buckeyes, 41–14, to win the national championship with a 13-1 record.

And just think, it might not have happened without Peyton Manning.

"Peyton Manning helped me a lot before the 2006 season," Leak said.

Say that again?

"Peyton, he helped me read defenses," Leak said. "I sat with him, picked his brain for a week at the Manning passing camp; we talked a lot when I went there to Louisiana. I learned a lot from him that week just talking about quarterback play."

The Tennessee people know about that?

"You mean, me being a Gator and he went to Tennessee, and we're supposed to hate each other?" Leak said. "Well, maybe, I don't know if they know or not. It was a quarterback helping a quarter-back." Leak thought about it a moment. "Peyton Manning, who was a Tennessee Vol, helped the Florida Gators win a national championship. I guess that did happen."

That same 2006 summer, in a federal courtroom in Atlanta, a marketing representative for Coca-Cola went on trial for trying to sell Coke secrets to Pepsi. This was the same thing, wasn't it? A Vol selling secrets to a Gator?

Leak laughed about this treachery. "This is how the quarterback fraternity works. It had nothing to do with being a Gator. They invited me down there. Every time I see Peyton today, we have a conversation about football. That's the thing about the quarterback fraternity, you help each other."

Vol fans will have to accept his word for it and try to get over the dot of orange that was inside the brain of Chris Leak, one of only three Florida quarterbacks in 105 seasons to lead the Gators to a national championship.

Manning, who finished at Tennessee in 1997, is the quarterback's quarterback. He studies defenses and mind-reads at presnap and postsnap. He knows where to go with the ball.

The Vol quarterback and Gator quarterback talked defense without regard for school colors. They talked about deciphering combination coverages, sorting out the defense, and making it pay.

"You have to take it one play at a time," Leak said. "You have to see if the corners are cheating up or back, if linebackers are shifted, if the defensive line is in a certain front."

Leak had built a solid relationship with head coach Urban Meyer in 2005 when he asked Meyer to add some more power to the spread with a fullback. Now, going into the 2006 season, Leak was ready to ask for something else thanks to Manning. Leak wanted to take not one, but three plays to the line of scrimmage. If the defense gave him a certain look, he wanted to have options.

"I was able to handle a lot, presnap and postsnap, and Coach Meyer did let me start calling three plays in the huddle," Leak said. "Peyton and I talked about everything. Presnap decisions, things about being in the shotgun, what he sees, what his checks are, and that's what got me confident going to the line with three plays. Obviously everyone knows how good Peyton is presnap and he taught me a lot.

"We would call three plays in the huddle and I would have five in my head. I prided myself in not being fooled by the defense. I wanted to handle a lot. Going to New Orleans and spending that week with Peyton was big for me and the Florida program."

All of it came together for Leak in 2006. It was his team, even with the future star, Tim Tebow, standing on the sidelines. Tebow had his package of plays in the spread, but the SEC was no place for a freshman quarterback, not even this freshman quarterback. Leak completed 63 percent of his passes as a senior. He moved the ball around, mostly to five different receivers. Manning had schooled him well, but there were also those countless hours he'd spent with his father, Curtis, in Charlotte, throwing and studying the position.

The Manning camp, which has been going on for seventeen years, usually includes the top college quarterbacks from around the country each summer. Leak showed up, but he always wore the same Florida T-shirt that week. Everyone else would wear a Manning-camp T-shirt.

Cooper Manning, Peyton and Eli's brother, chided Leak in a gathering of quarterbacks after camp, "Now we know Florida doesn't buy its players because Chris Leak wore the same shirt for four straight days."

Leak also showed up for camp with a truckload of questions. Each quarterback was allowed a private session with the Mannings, but Leak would get a question in whenever he could outside those sessions. He was a reporter chasing a story, getting one more tidbit, one more morsel.

"He was the nicest kid," Archie Manning said of Leak. "Peyton said he had plenty of questions, plenty of them."

Urban Meyer called Archie Manning and asked that Leak be toughened up for the fourth quarter and taught some leadership skills. Dan Mullen, the Florida offensive coordinator, called Manning and said, "Work with him on closing out games in the fourth quarter."

"After they won the national championship, I called Urban back and left a message for him, asking him, 'How did we do?' " Manning said.

The Mannings did just fine, and so did Leak.

Leak left Florida the career leader in passing attempts (1,458) and completions (895). That was mostly in two seasons under Urban Meyer (2005, 2006), but Leak gives a lot of credit to Zook for preparing him as a freshman and a sophomore. He finished his career completing 61.4 percent of his passes and is the all-time Florida leader in passing yards (11,213).

"All of us seniors when we came together after the game, we sat in the locker room and said, 'Mission accomplished.' Florida was back.

"Nobody panicked after the loss to Auburn that season. We went through a lot of peaks and valleys together. We just kept on. Nobody lost focus. We all kept saying it was our time, it was our season. We had that loss, but we kept going."

Leak thought for a moment how that season unfolded. For him, it started with the Manning passing camp. "Whenever I see Peyton, I remind him of that and how much it helped our team," Leak said.

Following its win over Arkansas in the SEC Championship Game and USC's loss to UCLA, Florida squeezed past No. 3 Michigan in the final BCS standings .9451 to .9317 to get a chance to play Ohio State for the national title. The Gators were lucky, but then they were too good for the Buckeyes, and it was the first SEC championship in this string of six straight titles.

CHAPTER 9

BIG PEOPLE DID BIG THINGS

Gus Malzahn, the Auburn offensive coordinator, held a laminated chart in his hands on the sidelines in 2010. It looked like the chart all OCs hold on the sideline. They flip it over, and flip it over again. They hold it close to their nose to see the fine print, and they refer to it for sixty minutes when calling plays. But here's a secret. Malzahn's card was not a play-calling chart. This was something different.

Malzahn was actually holding a slot machine.

He would look at that play chart, speak into his headset, then hand-signal the field. He might as well have been yanking the lever on a Vegas one-armed bandit because who knew what was coming out. Things were in a whir with Malzahn's version of the spread offense. He and his players knew what was coming out, but no one else did.

A running back might squat behind a guard and take the ball and dash around the left end. There were double passes, and there were passes off a reverse. It could be four receivers to one side, or it could be the quarterback going out for a pass. Other teams had trick plays, but Auburn just shrugged when it ran what appeared to be a gadget play. It was just part of the offense. Some plays were the same plays just gimmicked up to look different and make the defenders' heads spin as if they were inside that slot machine. Sometimes it was like putting the ball under a shell and moving it lickety-split. Coach Gadget Malzahn had it all.

Then, in the fourth game of the 2010 season, against South Carolina in Jordan-Hare Stadium, one play started coming out of the Malzahn slot machine more often than others. Lee Ziemba, the Tigers' left tackle, would line up on the right side for an unbalanced line. Center Ryan Pugh would snap the ball to quarterback Cam Newton, standing five yards back in this wildcat formation, and as Newton's fingertips touched the ball, left guard Mike Berry pulled out to the right side. Suddenly all the Auburn blockers were across the face of the defense to the play side of the field. Pugh was turning to his left and fielding for the pulling guard—that is, he was cutting off backside pursuit.

Now the ball was in the hands of a 250-pound quarterback, Newton, and roughly 1,500 pounds of rascally football players were bearing down against one side of the defense. The ground tilted.

"Without that play," said Jeff Grimes, the Auburn offensive line coach, "we wouldn't have won the national championship."

That Wildcat Power play in 2010 was a noxious animal to defenses. In other words, a beast. Newton ran for 176 yards and 3 touchdowns in the South Carolina game. The marquee lit up all over town and all over the SEC. Auburn had a king again, somebody that reminded the old folks of you know who. No one dared say it out loud, of course, but Newton was climbing onto the same pedestal as Bo Jackson.

Newton, who is 6-foot-6, is thick enough to block for himself because he hits defenders with shoulder pads first or a stiff arm. That power play kept drives alive on third and short. That play scored touchdowns in the red zone. That play gave Auburn something to rely on when they really needed positive yardage.

"You have to be good at something," Grimes said. "That's what we hung our hat on. We ended up making that a bigger piece of what we were doing. We knew we were going to run [Newton] some, but I think we saw a couple of things. We saw how good he was. We saw we were going to have to use him because we weren't dominant enough in other positions to hand the ball off or let him throw it. We needed him to run the ball against the better defenses we were going to see."

"That play couldn't be stopped," Pugh said.

That play also allowed the speedster halfback Onterrio Mc-Calebb, the fastest man on the field in some games, to take the ball on a jet sweep when Newton had the option to read the defensive end. If the end crashed to tackle Newton and shut down that power play, Newton was handing it to McCalebb, who was running flat to the sideline, and off he went because the defense had no sideboard. The end was tackling Newton.

Two touchdowns were scored against LSU's defense off those plays, the power and the read, with McCalebb going 70 yards on one carry. The Tigers blistered LSU for 440 yards rushing. It was the most rushing yards LSU had ever given up in a game.

Those plays were gold for Auburn, which went 14-0 and claimed the SEC's fifth consecutive national championship and the Tigers' first national championship since 1957. The power by Newton controlled the clock. It forced teams to play zone pass defense, not man-to-man, because you didn't want defenders turning their back on Newton in case he left the pocket. Defensive lines could not twist; they had to be sound so Newton could not escape the pocket easily.

The Newton power run established a culture of run intimidation. It also evened the game up. Auburn might not have been as talented on offense as other teams in the SEC, except when Newton tucked the ball and ran. When he ran with the ball, there was no better offense in the SEC.

"Several college coaches called me about that play and said they wanted their quarterback to run it," Grimes said. "After I talked to them about it, they said, 'I don't know if my quarterback is physical enough for that play.' That's the thing about the play. Your quarterback better be thick and he better be tough and he better be able to take a beating."

The Tigers averaged 284.8 yards per game rushing. It wasn't close to Alabama's 1973, wishbone-generated, SEC-record 366.1 yards per game rushing, but when you added the Tigers' passing numbers, 214.4 yards per game, well, you had a spectacle. Auburn set an SEC record with 6,989 offensive yards in 2010 on its way to the perfect record and a national championship. The Tigers were merely eighth in scoring defense (24.1 points allowed) in the conference, but they blistered teams with 41.2 points per game. A defense had to defend the fastest guy on the field, McCalebb, or the most athletic, Newton.

"We were fast-paced, up-tempo, and that limited some defenses," Grimes said. "Teams got really nervous about Cam breaking contain and running with the football, so you didn't see many inside moves, many line games where the end comes inside and the tackle comes around. It made our tackles' jobs easier in pass protection, and we ended up taking advantage of that. We set wide to those guys knowing they were not going to come with many inside moves."

That power/read option play, with that oversize quarterback and veteran offensive line, added a notch in the SEC belt with the win over Oregon in the National Championship Game. It was big people doing business on the football field, winning games from the inside out, tackle to tackle, against the Ducks, who ran a slimmer version of the spread. Oregon was not hefty enough to deal with Goliath.

Newton was not Goliath. The whole operation was Goliath.

Not only were the Auburn offensive linemen of decent size (304 pounds average among the five), they had been around the block as blockers. Ziemba was a senior and the left tackle. Berry was a senior and the left guard. Pugh was a senior and the center. Lee Isom was a senior and the right guard. Brandon Mosley, who took over at right tackle three games into the season for the injured A. J. Green, was the youngest lineman and he was a junior. As much as Tommy Tuberville was put down by athletic department staff for supposedly slacking off in recruiting his last season as head coach at Auburn, these were his guys, his legacy to Auburn beyond the undefeated team in 2004.

Then there was Grimes, the position coach, who learned offensive line play from, among others, the Philadelphia Eagles head coach Andy Reid. Grimes is a big guy, a Texas guy. Listen to the message on his voice mail. It is a deep, gravely, I-mean-business kind of voice.

"Hit until the echo of the whistle and be brawlers, that's who we were, that's what he taught us," Pugh said. "We wanted teams to turn on the film and know we were going to be the difference in the game. You ask Cam if he could have won the Heisman without us.

"We played 167 games together. We weren't the most talented. There was one guy among us seniors who was drafted, and that was in the seventh round. We played the game for each other."

It looked like it was all Newton, didn't it? He was fast and elusive and he was a quarterback who wasn't afraid to hit a tackler first. There is a lasting image of Newton lowering his shoulder and lowering the boom on the 216-pound Arkansas linebacker Jerico Nelson at the goal line at Jordan-Hare Stadium in 2010. Newton was 250 pounds and had a running start on Nelson, who was a good player.

Marcell Dareus, the Alabama tackle and first-round draft pick, brought Newton down by himself once on a bootleg. I don't remember another occasion when Newton was tackled by one man.

It sure didn't happen in preseason camp before the 2010 campaign. Newton had coaches as bodyguards and he wore the orange jersey that screamed *Hands off* the quarterback, especially this quarterback. The Tigers would run their spread plays during preseason camp throughout August against the defense, then watch the film to see how things were setting up for the season. Nobody was allowed to lay a hand on Newton and risk injury, which is the protocol in other programs, too, when it comes to the quarterback, but it was especially true in this program.

"You getting tackled here, Cam?" Gus Malzahn would say to Newton in the offense's meeting room as it reviewed film.

"Nope, not this time," the Auburn quarterback said.

Malzahn took the film forward. "Here, Cam?" the offensive coordinator said.

"Not here."

A little farther along in the film, Malzahn said, "Here, Cam?"

"I'm good here, Coach." Cam Newton was still on his feet in the film.

As long as Newton had the quarterback's bulletproof vest on, that orange-colored jersey, he was untouchable. The frothing defense wanted to hit him, put him on the ground, but the whistle always blew before Newton could be decked. It wasn't Newton they wanted to cream; he was just the guy with the ball.

"Can you imagine what would have happened if one time they didn't blow the whistle in camp," Pugh said, "and Cam got hit and was injured? Coach Chiz always had the whistle."

The coach who didn't blow the whistle before a fatal hit that August would have been plopped in the jail cell next to Harvey Updyke, the man who allegedly poisoned the trees at Toomer's Corner. There would have been a mob, an inquisition. Nobody would have found out just how good Cam Newton was with the football because he would be leaning on crutches on the sideline. All the ink would have been spared and there would have been none of the hand-wringing and regret over the scandal wrought by his father's asking for money from Mississippi State. None of it would have happened if Auburn had been careless, then unlucky, and Newton got a knee bent the wrong way in preseason camp.

So nobody hit Cam Newton in August. They all had an idea from the looks of him on the practice field that he might be productive because he was 6-foot-6, 250 pounds. Georgia recruited him as a tight end out of Atlanta, and he sure looked the part of an in-line blocker.

So, they kept asking themselves questions as they walked off the practice field in August. In the real game, with the spotlight on, could Cam twist out of tackles, could he bait the end on the option and duck inside and run for a mile? No one knew Newton was going to snatch the Heisman and have one of the greatest seasons ever in college football.

"We didn't know in preseason," Pugh said. "Nobody knew what was coming."

So Newton stayed upright all of preseason camp because of a whistle, and then, as no one could have envisioned, he stayed upright a good bit in the regular season, too.

Newton ran for 105.2 yards per game, 1,473 for the season. It was a rampage. Newton led the SEC in rushing and scored 20 touchdowns. He set Auburn records for total offense and scoring in one season. Newton did not have that orange vest on, but he had something just as protective as that preseason whistle: that veteran offensive line. Newton turned out to be pretty good, but so did his offensive line, which was practically invisible to the public outside Auburn with Newton filling up the picture frame and hoarding the spotlight.

Grimes and his guys were content with that. The coach would read to his linemen out of his book on the Spartans, the ancient warriors, and incite them to maul people on Saturdays and play together. They played hit-and-run football inside the Malzahn slot machine because it was a no-huddle offense and the ball was snapped every twenty seconds.

Grimes worked every day at making sure his linemen knew their assignments and did not give the defense a break by turning loose a linebacker by mistake. The double-team tandems always knew whom they were working so there would be no negative plays. Grimes has two degrees in education, so he taught and he taught. There was a hat on a hat in the blocking scheme. When you have playmakers, you have to make sure they can make plays by blocking the right people.

There's a problem with the no-huddle. There's no time to trash-talk. Ziemba couldn't spit out a quick enough crack at his teammates or opponents, but Pugh could chirp all day, and so could Berry. If one of the five missed an assignment, after a few seconds of berating the offender, it was on to the next play. If an opponent got clobbered, Pugh would pile on with smack. They were so busy jabbering and hustling into position for the next snap they didn't even have time to enjoy their work on the JumboTron.

"I looked up once at the previous play, which went for a big gain, and got yelled at," Pugh said. "We were moving fast . . . we learned how to trash-talk on the run."

Pugh always called the signals on the road, Newton at home, because you cannot hear on the road in the SEC. Sometimes the Tigers could walk to the line and almost announce the play loud and clear and the opponent still couldn't stop it. It would be third-and-short, or the Tigers would be in the red zone and Ziemba, the left tackle, lined up on the right side, and here came Goliath, Newton and the line, on that Wildcat Power run.

Alabama stopped it for a half in the 2010 Iron Bowl, but the Tigers just ran a zone play with Michael Dyer and started moving the ball in the second half. No other opponent that season had much luck with the power and the read off it.

"We started running inside zone against Bama," Pugh said. "We hadn't majored in that all year. We had majored in the gap scheme. Toward the end of the season everyone was overplaying our gap scheme so hard and the quarterback run so hard, we had to get to something else. That's why Dyer was able to have some success at the end of the year, because we were going to some inside-zone running that was tailored to him a little better and not so much the speed sweep and power running with Cam. Everyone was squeezing our power so hard we had to do something to move them vertically to get a seam."

But that signature play, the tackle over, and Newton's plowing, won a title for the Tigers. Newton got a statue in front of Jordan-Hare, but maybe there should have been a phalanx of blockers around him, statues of blockers, to show just how it was done that season.

"You know where the ball is going," said Todd Grantham, the Georgia defensive coordinator. "Alabama played them just like we played them, but we just couldn't get the guy [Newton] down. The first touchdown he had was the tackle-over formation. You saw it coming. You try and anchor with big men at those double-team points. You've got to be able to anchor. When they get movement at that point, it creates a seam in your defense and here he comes, 250 pounds."

Defenses said the same thing about Tebow, the wishbone fullback, when the Gators got in the red zone or in short yardage.

Here he comes.

Really, though, it should have been "Here *they* come." The 2008 Gators, who beat Oklahoma for the national championship, wore the same disguise as Auburn's 2010 champions. A spread-offense team that looked as if it had all kinds of clever plays and gadgetry and wanted to trick you, but was really an unpleasant group of people that wanted to knock you down, not go around.

The Florida offensive line featured Mike Pouncey, a guard taken in the first round of the 2011 NFL draft by the Miami Dolphins, and Maurkice Pouncey, a center, who was drafted in the first round of the 2010 draft by the Pittsburgh Steelers. There was left tackle Phil Trautwein, undrafted in 2009, but in the New Orleans Saints camp in 2012.

Jason Watkins, the right tackle, was undrafted in 2009, but stuck around in the camp of the Buffalo Bills for three years. Jim Tartt, a senior, was supposed to be the starter at left guard, but was limited to two starts because of recurring shoulder pain. Carl Johnson, a sophomore, started nine games at left guard in 2008. Marcus

Gilbert was a sophomore reserve on the 2008 team. He was drafted in the second round in 2011 by the Steelers.

Some ridicule was always coming from somewhere about the offensive line and Urban Meyer's spread offense. Sometimes that ridicule came from people who should know better, NFL scouts. They would label the Gators "elephant left" or "elephant right," which meant it was just big people ambling to one side or the other, not with power, but just girth, and getting in the way of defenders long enough for the fliers, Percy Harvin or Chris Rainey or Jeff Demps, to scoot by for big gains.

"People who say that, well, it's like me commenting on the space shuttle," Meyer said. "They don't know. We run gap schemes and we run zone schemes. Whoever makes that comment has no concept of what they're talking about. There are different kinds of spreads. Ours is off-tackle power and zone. It's an aggressive, physical spread.

"Our practices were some of the toughest in the country. We were a tough, rugged outfit. The people we played knew better. Our kids knew better."

Meyer still remembers gathering his offense with ten minutes left in the National Championship Game with Oklahoma in January 2009. He stared right into the eyes of his linemen and told them that if the Gators controlled the football, controlled the line of scrimmage, for at least seven minutes and could score, they would win the title. Florida led 17–14 and went 76 yards in 6:52 and scored. The Gators won, 24–14. The line was physical and plowed and plowed.

"We resented that talk we were a finesse team; people said that just because our offense was a spread formation," said Mickey Marotti, the Florida strength coach for the 2006 and 2008 national champions. "Absolutely we resented it, and it gave us a chip on our shoulder. The way we practiced and the way we trained, the one thing you saw was power football."

You could see the physical nature of the offense with Tebow coming downhill with the football in a vise grip of those thick arms. Tebow ran it 176 times for 673 yards that season and was the fullback every spread offense needs to keep the defense honest in the middle of the field. Tebow never, ever, ran wide to elude. It was all downhill into the teeth of the defense. The offensive line adored him. They called him Jesus and it did no good for him to protest such exaltation. He just smiled and went along with their fun.

"I remember riding the bus to the Oklahoma game, the one for the championship, and I was sitting with the Pounceys and Tim," Watkins said. "Well, Tim tells this horrific joke. It was really bad. We all laughed anyway. If Jesus is telling a joke, you better laugh."

On the hot, muggy days in Gainesville, the offensive line would turn to Tebow and ask him to "call God and get some wet down here so it wasn't so hot and we wouldn't pass out."

Watkins was the right tackle and protected Tebow's blind side. "Got to take care of Jesus, baby," he said. "Man, you don't let Jesus get hit from behind."

But just like Auburn with Newton, the Gators offense was more than Tebow. It was that offensive line, too. They were maulers because of offensive line coach Steve Addazio, and there was nothing finesse about him. Watkins still remembers those occasions when one of the Florida linemen would take one wrong step on a play, one measly wrong step, and Addazio would erupt and make the whole unit take a bunch of steps . . . thousands of them, right up to the top of the ninety-thousand-seat football stadium.

"Nobody liked him at first," Watkins said. "I didn't like him. He would get on us bad. But . . . he turned us into maulers. He got on the scholarship guys and then the walk-ons. One messes up, we all ran. You get tired of the up-downs and you get tired of doing stadiums. You see how big our stadium is? Ninety thousand. It's a big, big place, and we had to run up those stands."

Addazio demanded precise footwork on that line. He never let his guys get away with using talent and strength. If he were to put down a large piece of paper under them on the field with all the correct steps mapped out, Addazio would expect them to step exactly into those spaces with those big feet.

"We had a lot of power runs and gap plays," Watkins said. "We had to do it right. You couldn't just run over people. You had to have the proper technique."

Pugh, the Auburn center, said he and his teammates studied that 2008 Florida offensive line. The scheme was similar, and so were the quarterbacks, so the Tigers tried to pick up a few things from the Gators. It was instant admiration for the toughness, and the talent that went with it.

"They were really talented, you could see it on film," Pugh said. "The Pounceys were really good, first-rounders, I think. They were something to watch. It helped us watching that whole O-line because we ran some similar plays."

The offensive linemen that blocked for Tebow in 2008 also blocked some for Newton, who was the Gators' third-string quarterback that season. Newton left Florida following the 2008 season and enrolled in Blinn junior college. He said he left because Tebow was coming back for his senior season, but the *New York Times* reported Newton left because he was about to be brought before a university committee on discipline for multiple cases of cheating.

Watkins and Trautwein had no problems with classes. Watkins took a degree in education. Trautwein did enough work to get a master's. Meyer was a nag when it came to classwork. Although Florida had many discipline issues, the O-line managed itself well, with an exception or two.

"The smartest thing I did at Florida was that I was not going to hang around just sports people," Watkins said. "The people on the academic side of the campus were going to be the CEOs, so I hung out with them and the athletic types. I wanted to surround myself with those academic folks, so I branched out. It can be a problem just hanging out with athletic types; so you want to mix in and meet other people. I got a lot out of my education because of that. Trautwein got his master's, so you know we had some serious people off the field."

On the field, it was serious business, too, especially with Tebow. The players looked at him and chided that his sculpted body was not real. "That's a mannequin, that's not Tim," Watkins said.

The offense fit together—Tebow and the offensive line—because of the speed element also, the scare-masters, Harvin, Demps, and Rainey, who scored from anywhere on the field. When you mixed in the power inside, the speed became faster.

Meyer said the team's best play was a counter to Harvin. He would line up as an H-back to the right side, take a quick step to the right, then flash back left for a handoff from Tebow. That quick step right was enough to make linebackers, or a defensive line, reactively step with Harvin, which was away from the play. Before the linebackers or D-end knew it, an offensive lineman was on their inside shoulder pushing them away from the center of the play, where Harvin was headed with the football. Harvin averaged 9.4 yards a carry and scored 10 rushing touchdowns that season.

"We cut them off and, with Percy, that was all he needed," Watkins said. "You just needed a little gap. They are reading him. His footwork is setting up our blocks and gives us more angles."

Said Meyer, "He had the best first step in college football."

The power play with a speed guy was done out of a spread formation. Offensive linemen were driving defensive linemen into the laps of linebackers. There was nothing finesse about it. Six hundred pounds were on three hundred pounds. One Gator would hold up that three-technique defensive tackle, then another Gator would come from another angle to move him. Six hundred pounds can move three hundred pounds.

"Coach Addazio wanted you to take that down lineman backward, that's basically what he wanted you to do, and that way you are giving the running back enough room to work with," Watkins said. "That's power right there."

The only defensive lineman the Gators did not drive off the ball was Terrence Cody, Alabama's 400-pound nose tackle.

"Now that was one guy that was just not fair to deal with," Watkins said. "Almost four hundred pounds tipping over. Not moving that guy. He was just an anchor. You just run away from him because he's not going to catch anybody."

The Gators used power to set up finesse. You know that goofy-looking Pop Pass Tebow used to throw to the 6-foot-6 tight end Tate Casey at the goal line? It was set up by two power plays on first and second down. On the third play, the Gators would block again as if it were a power play, except this time Tebow would jump and throw that downhill balloon to Casey for the touchdown.

What about the shovel pass to the tight end Hernandez? It was a power play, too, gap blocking all the way, Meyer said. Florida was leading undefeated Alabama, 24–20, in the fourth quarter of the

2009 SEC Championship Game and had a first down at the Tide's 21-yard line when Addazio called for the shovel pass to Hernandez. It went for 15 yards to the Bama 6. The Gators scored and won 31–20.

"How the blocking was formed up depended on what look the defense gave us," Watkins said. "If it was six in the box, it was one play; if we came to the line and it was seven in the box, it was another play. Read the defense, read the defense. Six in the box we ran the shovel to Hernandez. He could line up in split backs, slot back, or end, or we could move him in motion to give it a different look, but it was the shovel."

It looked like a complex play and it was, but nothing about how the play was called was complex.

"Shovel pass," Watkins said. "That's what Tim said in the huddle. That's all. He would say, 'Shovel pass.' Same thing with Pop Pass. He would just call, 'Pop Pass.' When you have a lot of plays, well, with some of our guys you got to be point-blank and say 'shovel,' and that's the play. I'm not knocking 'em, but you had to spell it out and be point-blank with some of them about what the play was.

"I'll tell you something else. For that shovel play to be stopped, we must have messed up something."

Florida's 2008 offensive line lived by the same mandate as Auburn's 2010 offensive line. You had to be together to run the ball. The spread plays looked extravagant and full of fancy and a coach's artwork, but that wasn't all there was to it. The Gators up front used pure muscle to be the castle builders for Tebow and Harvin when it came to the run game.

"You live by running the ball in football," Watkins said. "We had all the plays, but it takes five guys on one chord to run the ball, and the one thing we wanted to do more than anything was hurt the feelings of the defensive coach on the other team by running the football. He hates to give up yards on the ground. Any of those defensive coaches hate it. Makes them sad when they look at the stat sheet and see his guys gave up a bunch of yards rushing.

"If we had a running game one Saturday that our coach wasn't proud of, trust me, we were going to do inside drills until we couldn't do them anymore. We had to run the football with power for us not to have to do those drills."

The Gators averaged 6 yards a carry. The one bad game they had running the football was the second game of the season, a 26–3 win over Miami, where Florida gained just 89 yards rushing. It was a classic gang-up at the line to see if Tebow could win the game with the pass. He did. Tebow completed 21 of 35 passes for 256 yards and 2 touchdowns.

The most disappointing play of the season was at home against Ole Miss. The Gators were down 31–30 and faced fourth-and-1 with less than a minute to play at the Rebels 32. Tebow was in the shotgun perhaps just to give him a running start for that yard. He got stacked up at the line by Ole Miss defensive tackle Peria Jerry, who became a first-round draft pick of the Atlanta Falcons. It was no gain and a stunning loss, the only loss of the season for Florida.

Tebow begged for forgiveness from his teammates, but it wasn't necessary. They all knew he was tough enough.

Meyer still marvels over that 2008 team. It was all about complementary football, offense and defense, and special teams. The Gators averaged 43 points a game and gave up 12 points a game. They had a dangerous return man in Brandon James, and the Gators' special teams had blocked 8 kicks going into the National Championship Game against Oklahoma in Miami.

"It was one of the most balanced teams I have ever seen," Meyer said. "We were beating teams by twenty and thirty points, and this was inside the SEC, the best conference in the country."

CHAPTER 10

NO CUTTING IN LINE

Jan. 5, 2009

To: mhamilton@tennessee.edu

Mike, I do hope you budgeted extra money for NCAA
violations defense expenses. Keep this website handy.
http://www.tcgathletics.com.

Jan. 5

From: Hamilton, Michael Edward

We haven't received penalties for a major violation
since the 80s, so we're not planning on changing that
now . . . we have a proactive compliance program. Go
Vols—Mike

Jan. 23, 2009

To: mhamilton@tennessee.edu

The athletic department is out of control.

Feb. 16, 2009

To: mhamilton@tennessee.edu

Someone from the coaching staff over at the UT circus has been in discussions with the athletic director at [REDACTED] High School. The AD didn't quite understand what the coach was selling/telling him; he was too shocked at hearing a Tennessee football coach recommend that a high school kid drop out of school before graduating . . . this gambit would somehow get the kid an extra year of eligibility.

Feb. 16, 2009

To: mhamilton@tennessee.edu

Subject: Maybe nip this one in the bud

17.02.13 is clearly being violated (probably as I type this)

Feb. 27, 2009

To: mhamilton@tennessee.edu

Subject line: "If you ain't cheating, you ain't trying."

Mike . . . Players are being asked to falsely affirm the number of hours they practice each week.

Mike Hamilton, the University of Tennessee athletic director, would find these e-mails from his staff in his in-box routinely in the winter of 2009. Lane Kiffin, his football coach, was a tireless recruiter and was going to prove to be a masterful play-caller, but Hamilton's staff inside the Stokely Athletic Center thought the thirty-three-year-old coach was in too much of a hurry to get his own national championship trophy. Kiffin had the Vols hooked to his fast sled, which was to win now and challenge the Gators and Tigers and the rising Tide. Kiffin was trying to cut in line.

Hamilton had his hands full. Kiffin was ticking off one secondary NCAA violation after another while Bruce Pearl, the basketball coach, was bringing heat on the department for a violation and then lying to the NCAA about it. Pearl was eventually fired.

Kiffin, who had been hired to replace Phil Fulmer, quit January 12, 2010, after one season, a 7-6 campaign in 2009, which ended with a 37–14 thumping at the hands of Virginia Tech in the Chick-fil-A Bowl. The night Kiffin quit, T-shirts were burned on campus, and their charred remains lay in the gutter the next morning. Students were angry at the coach who vowed to get Tennessee back on the same level as Florida and Urban Meyer but bolted for the head coaching job at Southern California. But inside Stokely Athletic Center, where the UT athletic offices were located, there was some rejoicing. Kiffin was gone. Good riddance, many thought to themselves.

Derek Dooley was hired as head coach January 15, 2010.

Some perceived that Kiffin was just doing his part to uphold what was viewed as a culture of rule-bending in the Southeastern Conference. It is supposed to be the Wild West with the familiar phrase being uttered, "It is better to beg forgiveness than ask permission." But something was more ominous about Kiffin's style, something worse than bending a few rules. The old-school Tennessee fans, including staffers on campus, saw Kiffin sneer at UT traditions. SEC fans rally around traditions, and like them or not, they help fuel the passion, which fills the bank accounts of the successful program. That was Kiffin's big misstep around Knoxville. He got on the wrong side of Old Smokey.

He also got on the wrong side of the other coaches in the SEC. In February 2009, Kiffin accused Florida coach Urban Meyer of cheating, then backed down and apologized. Kiffin's mirror must have been broken. He was the one cheating. He was accused of six secondary violations of NCAA rules, which included disclosing the name of an unsigned recruit on Twitter and setting up press conferences with a photographer present to impress recruits.

Headline writers around the SEC had a good time with the Tennessee coach. He was called Boy Blunder and Lane Violation. That was too bad because Kiffin can coach and could recruit, but it was all obscured by missteps and spitting on some sacred Tennessee traditions. It wasn't just the loyalists of fired coach Phil Fulmer who had it in for Kiffin; others around the department thought the rookie college head coach had way too much swagger.

Kiffin had come from the Oakland Raiders, fired by Al Davis, who was assumed to be a reckless owner. After a few months on campus, Kiffin was giving the impression that he was reckless, that he had deserved to be pushed out at Oakland, that Davis was not such a kook after all.

Hamilton and his compliance officers made attempts to keep Kiffin under control and within the boundaries of the NCAA rulebook. One of the department's compliance officers went out to football practice on February 17, 2009, and coaches suddenly disappeared from a 7-on-7 "voluntary" workout. According to NCAA rules, the coaches were not allowed to be present with footballs before spring practice began.

But according to sources, the coaches reappeared, so did the footballs.

One former player, who did not want to be identified, said spring practices did not begin in March, the legal starting date, but on crisp February mornings.

Here are some more e-mails from staff members to Hamilton:

Offensive meeting this afternoon . . . probably finished by now.
The meeting is to be followed by two different workouts—one

with the ball, one without. It is gray/borderline NCAA compliant at
best. 17.02.13 is clearly being violated (probably as I type this).

Mike . . . there is clearly some misunderstanding about the
number of hours players can be required to practice right now.
Someone needs to explain to the players the rules.

When the team is working on the defensive end of Haslam field,
someone is set up in the stairwell in Stokely with a camera. They
film from inside the stairwell, through a glass window, across
the street. It just raises the question, "If filming these workouts is
permissible, why not use one of the towers? Why hide to do it?

Brad Bertani, the associate athletics director for compliance, said in an e-mail to Hamilton that he investigated some of the allegations by staff members. Bertani, who was hired at Ohio State in March 2012, said he was present during a football conditioning drill on Monday, February 16, 2009, and no balls or coaches were present. Bertani said there were no formations and no play-calling. He also told Hamilton he warned UT assistant coaches they could not be present.

It did not stop the e-mails to Hamilton from his staff inside Stokely.

One of the more serious e-mails came from a staff member to Hamilton on February 27, 2009:

Within the last 10 days he [Kiffin] invited a parent to practice.
The parent responded, "I didn't know practice had started yet."
Coach Kiffin responded, "Well, we just have to keep moving so
the compliance people don't catch up with us."

Did Kiffin understand the rules? He was a new head coach in college football, but not new to the game. He had nine seasons as a college assistant coach. The NCAA manual is thick, sure, but he and his assistants were not just out of high school. The Tennessee coach spent his time recruiting and coaching and not reading the NCAA rulebook.

What was not excusable to some Vol fans was Kiffin's disregard for some traditions.

The day after Kiffin resigned as Tennessee coach, Josh McNeil, an offensive lineman recruited by Fulmer, said in a phone interview that Kiffin was disgracing the Tennessee traditions. McNeil said Kiffin was even debating the merits of the most sacred tradition, the Maxims, which are on a tall board inside the locker room. McNeil said the coach did not want them as part of his sermons to the team, which was Kiffin's right, but irresponsible to Big Orange faithful. The Maxims were Tennessee in-game prerequisites for winning that had survived since the hallowed days of the legendary coach General Robert Neyland.

McNeil refused requests for follow-up interviews because he did not want to say anything that would get "my school" in trouble. But on January 12, 2010, the day Kiffin resigned at Tennessee, McNeil unloaded on Kiffin in a long interview with former AOL columnist Clay Travis, who now runs the website Outkick the Coverage.

"They'd replaced our highlight video from the past season with Reggie Bush, Matt Leinart, and Dwayne Jarrett from USC. I was like, 'Man, I know we were five and seven last year, but this is Tennessee. Right beside our national title trophy? Come on, man.' "

McNeil told Travis that he walked up the stairs to the Neyland-Thompson Sports Center, and twenty televisions were mounted in the building that had still photos on the screen. The colors were not orange, they were red, USC red. There was a shot of Reggie Bush, the former USC back, diving into the end zone.

McNeil's face was the next red thing. "I was thinking, Damn, Jamal Lewis went here. Travis Henry went here. It ain't like we never had any running backs of our own," McNeil told Travis.

People around the facility commented that Kiffin wanted to turn Tennessee into the "USC of the South," forgetting that Tennessee had won a national title in 1998 under Kiffin's predecessor, Phil Fulmer.

McNeil finally had enough and confronted Kiffin, according to the AOL story: "Coach, I feel like you're intentionally not embracing UT's traditions."

Kiffin replied, "Well, whatever Tennessee's been doing isn't working anymore, so we're coming up with something new. Get used to it."

The references to the Trojans kept coming. On Junior Day, March 2, 2009, McNeil said Kiffin and his staff, which included the ace recruiters Lance Thompson and Ed Orgeron, had a large crop of potential recruits on Tennessee's campus. McNeil told Travis that players were divided into offensive and defensive players. They were seated for a video and told this was going to be how Tennessee played football.

A play featuring Reggie Bush came across the screen. More Southern Cal highlights followed.

McNeil said Kiffin did not take the Maxims on the road to games. Neyland had had his teams memorize them season after season. Kiffin abhorred the Maxims. Assistant coaches also did not repeat the Maxims.

"Coach Kiffin cared about Tennessee traditions less than the worst Vol hater in the state of Alabama," McNeil said. "That man's a snake."

McNeil, asked about his comments in the story after Kiffin resigned, said, "All true," before refusing to discuss the Kiffin era any further.

The Tennessee traditions might have seemed stale to Kiffin, but a coach who was an outsider to the program has to tread carefully. A large block of fans were still devoted to former coach Fulmer, a native of Tennessee. That block of fans had considerable influence in Knoxville, and when Kiffin rode into town with too much bravado, they were taken aback. Plenty of fans were tickled by his brashness, especially when it came to Florida and the other rivals, but Kiffin walked a fine line with former players.

"Lane Kiffin was a terrible hire for the University of Tennessee, but that was not his fault," said David Moon, a former UT player and a financial adviser in Knoxville. "You can't fault a skunk for smelling bad. But you can fault the guy who brings a pack of skunks in the house." It was a reference to Hamilton, the former Tennessee athletic director.

Even Mike Slive, the commissioner of the Southeastern Conference, a recovering lawyer who parses his words, got in a dig at Kiffin at the 2010 SEC Media Days. In his State of the SEC Address, Slive said, "The other head coaching change took place at Tennessee when Derek Dooley's predecessor left to return to his western roots [smiling]. I want to welcome Coach Dooley back to the SEC. And when I say 'welcome,' I mean welcome."

For a year, Slive and staff were following behind Kiffin, as if he were a reckless driver bouncing off parked cars. They were routinely investigating allegations of violations. Most of them were the minor indiscretions of a young coach who had just come from the NFL and was apparently not well versed on all the details of the rulebook, even though he had considerable experience in college football. That's what Kiffin said, anyway.

On April 29, 2009, staffers traded e-mails about Kiffin's knowledge of the rulebook, or lack of knowledge. Their names were redacted, but the subject line was not.

> Subject: The forgot to read the handbook
> *Coach Kiffin (the younger) was at Cincinnati Moeller High School last week working out a quarterback.*
>
> *This is a definite NCAA no-no. I suggest quizzing the AD about it.*

Then there was the e-mail dated February 18, 2009. The subject line was caustic: *And you thought they had gone 24 hours without a violation.* The staffer writes:

> *Monte Kiffin was present at yesterday's "voluntary" workout. Violation. These voluntary workouts are being filmed and evaluated. Violation.*

Anonymous e-mails from inside the Tennessee athletic department also found their way to Greg Sankey, associate commissioner of the Southeastern Conference. Kiffin was allegedly off campus during the off-campus dead period in recruiting for head coaches, working out a player in Cincinnati.

One violation did not seem so secondary. *New York Times* reporters Pete Thamel and Thayer Evans reported December 8, 2009, that hostesses from Tennessee's Spirit Squad, whose office was just down the hallway from Hamilton's, were in South Carolina holding up pro-Tennessee signs and actively recruiting several high school stars.

If true, it would be a clear NCAA violation, and would be especially serious if it could be proved that Kiffin had sent them there and, worse, used athletic department money to pay for the trip. Lacey Earps, one of the hostesses, works in the insurance field in Raleigh, North Carolina, and did not respond to a request to talk about her involvement in off-campus recruiting.

Something even more sinister was going on with the program when football players were arrested in an alleged holdup of a man outside of a Knoxville convenience store. It all seemed so out of control.

Kiffin was never charged with a major violation at Tennessee. In a statement from Los Angeles on August 24, 2011, Kiffin said, "I'm very grateful to the NCAA, the Committee on Infractions and its chairman, Dennis Thomas, for a very fair and thorough process. I'm also very grateful that we were able to accurately and fairly present the facts in our case and that no action was taken against us. I'm pleased that the NCAA based its decision on the facts and not on perception. I'm also very grateful that the Tennessee football program was cleared of any wrongdoing."

Certainly Kiffin is not the only SEC coach who has required a bar of soap. The promise of a haul of cash for winning in the SEC created some unsavory behavior. Alabama's Antonio Langham, the savior of the first SEC Championship Game, was not the only bad actor as the SEC built its brand. He was jaywalking compared to the others.

There were irregularities at Alabama when Mike DuBose was the coach. Then, Mike Price, who replaced Dennis Franchione following the 2002 season, was fired in May 2003 for a trip to a topless bar and the ensuing scandal.

An Alabama booster, Logan Young, was linked to the recruitment of Albert Means, a star defensive lineman in Memphis. The names of SEC schools were dragged through a courtroom as the FBI was brought into the case. Arkansas and Georgia were among the schools linked to Means, and the rest of the country cackled at the spectacle of the shameless SEC.

Alabama got hung up in a bookselling violation by football players. More recently, the Crimson Tide have apparently dodged trouble with their football players' association with a clothing retailer in Tuscaloosa. The websites Outkick the Coverage and Sports by Brooks turned up photograph after photograph of memorabilia signed by Alabama players being sold by T-Town Menswear. Alabama subsequently sent a letter to the store owner barring him from his place on the sidelines in Bryant-Denny Stadium. The letter was delivered only after reporting by the websites.

In 2009, a former LSU assistant coach, D. J. McCarthy, committed a major violation recruiting a junior college star. The Tigers self-reported, admitted guilt, and were placed on one-year probation. And the coach was fired. Quarterback Jordan Jefferson was in a bar fight and suspended in 2011. Defensive back and kick-return specialist Tyrann Mathieu was suspended for the use of synthetic marijuana, according to published reports.

The rest of college football has had its issues, too. North Carolina and Ohio State have been bagged by the NCAA recently. Miami's football program was associated with a brazen booster who showered benefits on players. Penn State and the child-abuse scandal was a four-month morality play of who-knew-what-when. Southern California could not play in a bowl game in 2011, which was too bad for the Trojans because they looked like a dangerous team at the end of the season.

In April 2012, the SEC was put to the test about its morals and integrity when Arkansas coach Bobby Petrino was caught having an affair with an employee and admitted to opening the door for her to get a job connected with the football program. It was another low-character move by Petrino, who walked out on the Atlanta Falcons before the end of the 2007 season. He had also tried to go in the back door to get the Auburn job while Tommy Tuberville, his former boss, was still the coach.

This time, Petrino was coaching a team with the SEC championship in its sights, and if you win the SEC championship, chances are you can compete for a national title. The Razorbacks were loaded with top ten talent going into the 2012 season, and Petrino, regarded as a master play-caller, had Arkansas on the doorstep again for national recognition.

He was fired.

Jeff Long, the Arkansas athletic director, consulted with Slive, the SEC commissioner. The message from Slive, according to G. David Gearhart, the Arkansas chancellor, was pretty direct. Fire him if you must, and the SEC will stand behind you. Never mind that Petrino should never have been hired by Arkansas in the first place given his behavior in Atlanta and with chasing the Auburn job.

The SEC needed Petrino to be ousted. Not only was he a bad actor, but if Petrino had remained in his job, it would have been a blight on the entire SEC. Suppose he had won the conference title—Alabama and LSU are home games for Arkansas in 2012—and had a crack at the seventh straight national championship for the SEC? Imagine the scorn from the rest of college football for keeping Petrino around to win games.

"The dismissal here of a topflight coach speaks to our commitment of doing things the right way," said Gearhart. "Jeff Long has never said anything about cutting corners. He's proven that the last couple of weeks.

"Jeff talked directly to Mike Slive and got advice from Mike Slive before any decision was made. Mike was one hundred percent on board. It was gratifying to hear from the head of the conference that, look, if you have a coach that isn't doing things the right way, then you've got to take action. I have always seen Mike as being very tough at obeying the rules."

Arkansas got it right when it fired Petrino, but then it hijacked a coach who had just started at Weber State, John L. Smith. So the Razorbacks deserve only so much applause. One can suppose that taking someone else's coach five months before the start of the season is life in the big city.

———

Slive, who became the SEC commissioner in 2002 when Kramer retired, vowed then to rid the SEC of cheating within five years. People snickered throughout the nine-state home of the conference, and elsewhere in college football, because the SEC had numerous compliance issues. Long ago, the SEC had lost the benefit of the doubt among media and fans, and people all over the SEC doubted that Slive had enough cleaning solution.

Slive inherited two NCAA cases in 2002, but he nearly fulfilled the five-year pledge. He didn't make it to five years not because of a violation in football, but because the Arkansas track team was caught breaking rules. Football stayed out of jail until the Alabama bookselling fiasco, and some thought that Slive wasn't looking under the right rocks.

"There may be the perception out there that we're the Wild Wild West, but it's not that way," said Fulmer, the former Tennessee coach.

Fulmer said that on occasion in his seventeen years at Tennessee, other coaches in a conference meeting asked the commissioner, either Kramer or Slive, to leave the room while a head coach was dressed down by his colleagues for violations.

"You pay the fiddler if you dance," Fulmer said. "There were times we got after a head coach if there were things that were going on. You deal with it on the front end, which was with the coaches."

Slive hammers on schools to follow the rules, no matter what the rest of college football wants to believe. He is viewed as a defense attorney for the bad actors in the SEC because of the lack of transparency in the conference with regard to rule-breaking. But in meetings with new coaches in Birmingham, Slive tells them all, "If you're caught cheating, I hope you're fired."

When Hamilton resigned as Tennessee athletic director in June 2011, he was right about football under his watch. It had no sanctions for major violations and no one was fired. The dirtiest deeds were done by the basketball coach, Pearl; and his assistants, who lied about their violations. But Hamilton was not under fire at Tennessee for Pearl alone. Kiffin, with his brashness and bold talk to get up to speed with Florida, which had won national championships in 2006 and 2008, and with his sudden departure, also greased the path for Hamilton's resignation.

————

Hamilton is currently president of U.S. Operations for Blood: Water Mission, a nonprofit organization based in Nashville that addresses Africa's clean-water and HIV/AIDS crises. He told the *Chattanooga Times Free Press* he had to leave Knoxville because of threats to his family.

"I received several threats and it reached a point that I moved my family out of Knoxville for several days last spring [2011] and I was even assigned police protection," Hamilton told the paper.

Hamilton told the newspaper that he and his wife have five young, adopted children, "so I had to stop and realize life is short and it was time to reassess my priorities."

The SEC, meanwhile, may yet have to deal with the ambitious Kiffin, perhaps as soon as the 2012 season. Southern California is off probation and laundered clean of the Reggie Bush/Pete Carroll affair, and they are reloading with blue-chippers. Southern California is about to reclaim its place among college football's elite because of Kiffin. On November 19, 2011, the Trojans went into Eugene, Oregon, and took down No. 4 Oregon, 38–35. Perhaps that's when quarterback Matt Barkley realized the potential for 2012 and decided to stay for another season at Southern Cal. He is the 2012 Heisman front-runner, perhaps the best quarterback in the country, and he will get a chance at whom? LSU, Alabama, Georgia? All three will have nasty defenses in 2012.

If not this season, then one season soon, Kiffin will get a chance to show the SEC, after all the rigmarole, that he was not just talk, that he may be the next great coach in college football.

CHAPTER 11

AWAKENING A GIANT II: SABAN AGAIN

2009, 2011

In Berea, Ohio, in the early spring of 1991, the Cleveland Browns started to piece together their system for evaluating college football players for the draft. The Browns wanted to develop a method in which one general manager evaluated players, but the Browns' GM would not be a man, but a grading system. Too many times, individual bias had crept into the draft room as scouts made a plea for "their guy." With set definitions of what the team wanted in players, position by position, and then a numerical value assigned to a player on how he fit those definitions, the process should yield better players. There would be uniformity even as the team changed scouts and front office personnel. The grade was the grade and that was that.

NFL teams had grading systems, sure, but grades for players could differ from scout to scout. In some systems nothing was hard-and-fast. So the Browns defined what they wanted in a player at each position and graded according to that. For instance, in 1991, the ideal size for a center was 6-foot-3, 280 pounds, with a 5.19-second

40-yard dash. The grade went up or down based on that height, weight, and speed definition.

The system the Browns began to devise played the percentages, declaring that a player of a certain height, weight, and speed was capable of a certain level of accomplishment in professional football. If a player met the requirements for his position, he remained on their list of draftable players. If the player did not fit the Cleveland prototype, he was downgraded with a letter or tag—*B* for "bulk," Z for "height," for instance—and then he had to be special in some other area.

The scouts would also fill in numerical values for each player's "critical factors," position by position, such as athletic ability, strength/explosion, and playing speed.

Finally, number grades were handed out and the players were placed on the draft board accordingly.

The organization held fast to their scouting creed because the heavy hand of Bill Belichick said that was how it was to be done.

Ernie Accorsi was the general manager for the Browns back in 1991, but the player decision-maker was Belichick, the head coach. Belichick did not start from scratch with this system. He flew in Gil Brandt, the former Dallas Cowboys general manager, who had devised a system of grading college football players that dated back to 1961, a system that had used supercomputers from Silicon Valley to calculate grades. When the Cowboys were putting together their system, they sought the expertise of college football coaches. They sent letters to fifty college coaches asking them for definitions and descriptions for the ideal player at every position. One of the coaches who helped significantly was Jerry Claiborne, the trusted assistant coach of Alabama and Texas A&M, and Alabama coach Bear Bryant.

Brandt and his own trusted right-hand man, Dick Mansberger, put together a computer-generated, two-hundred-page scouting manual, which has been copied as many times as people could get their hands on it. Scouts used to joke about the manual, "It told us everything, including how to go pee." Brandt sat for five meetings with Belichick and Michael Lombardi, who was pro personnel director, and Brandt allowed the Browns to inspect and dissect the Cowboys' system with question after question. The Browns then went about adding their own theories and expertise.

But more than Belichick and Lombardi did the tweaking. Ron Marciniak, a former Cowboys scout who was working with the Browns, shared his thoughts on scouting in Berea with Dom Anile, the Browns' college scouting director. Anile would take his own ideas for the system to Belichick and lay them out, sometimes while Belichick was on the treadmill in his office. At times a young assistant personnel man, Jim Schwartz, now the Detroit Lions' head coach, was also involved in "updating" the system. It was months and months of work, said Lombardi, who is now an analyst for NFL.com.

The meetings to develop a robust system of scouting college players eventually included Cleveland's offensive coordinator, Gary Tranquill, and the defensive coordinator, a guy just in from the college ranks at Toledo.

Nick Saban.

He was thirty-nine years old and on his ninth coaching job since leaving Kent State (1970–72), where he played defensive back. Saban helped with the refinement of the system in his three years with the Browns, and when he left Cleveland in 1994 to become the head coach at Michigan State, he took it with him. He carried it again to LSU in November 1999, then to the Miami Dolphins in

2004, and now it spins inside the heads of coaches and player personnel staff in Tuscaloosa.

The foundation of Alabama's recruiting is this player-evaluation system developed by the Browns, but with roots in Dallas that go back fifty years. The Crimson Tide grades high school players it is recruiting 1 through 5—the Browns system was 5 through 8—and this system not only helped Alabama win national titles in 2009 and 2011, it helped the Cowboys and Patriots and Baltimore Ravens win Super Bowls.

"I think, obviously, Nick came to the Browns in 1991 with a significant amount of knowledge, especially when it came to the actual coaching of the players and the schemes," said Phil Savage, the executive director of the Senior Bowl in Mobile, who used the system when he was the scouting director for the Baltimore Ravens and was the general manager of the Cleveland Browns. "Any college coach that comes to the NFL probably learns more about scouting and evaluation techniques, more than they ever knew when they were in college.

"I think Nick took the Browns' system and applied his own thoughts and his own philosophies to it once he got to Michigan State. I think he has modified it and improved it, and now he has been to two places, LSU and Alabama, where it all makes sense and it is a perfect marriage of being able to recruit the top players and those top players fitting the bill of what he is trying to get on the team."

What the system does best for Alabama is eliminate mistakes in recruiting. An Alabama assistant coach cannot look at a high school player and declare the player fit to play defensive line for the Crimson Tide if that player does not match the definitions of the position: height, weight, speed, and critical factors, such as athletic ability and strength/explosion. The system does not allow assistant coaches to be general managers and just put a player on the recruiting board for consideration. If the assistant coaches have too much say, you cannot run the Alabama/Cleveland scouting program. There is too much personal bias and then mistakes are made evaluating players.

All you had to do, Lombardi said, was look at the various draft "war rooms" on NFL draft night to see the potential for mistakes. These rooms were crowded with scouts and personnel men, people with opinions on players. It was not crowded in the New England Patriots' draft room, which was run by Saban's friend Belichick. No multitude of decision-makers were inside that room. In that small group of people the decision-maker was the system.

Brandt said the beauty of the system is grading the middle 80 percent of draftable players. A housewife could pick out the top 10 percent of players and the bottom 10 percent. Those players in the middle, that 80 percent, provide the challenge for NFL teams.

"You get more chances to win the lottery with a player," Brandt said of the system. "You get as many ways as you can to break the logjam with that middle eighty percent."

No scouting system is foolproof, but this system, Brandt said, allowed a history of performance to be the guide. Players of a certain height, weight, speed, and critical factors in playing a position were judged against similar players who had come before them. It is not quite football's version of Moneyball because the critical factors used to grade a player need a scout's eye. Moneyball seems to be based more on a projection of numbers only.

Anile said the big issue the NFL teams had to deal with before the draft was that the scout in the West, the scout in the Midwest, the scout in the South, and the scout in the East each had his own view of who could play offensive tackle in the NFL. If each of the four scouts graded guys in individual ways, the team might have thirty offensive tackles to choose from. Who was the best player? Under the Browns' system, everybody had to grade the same way. They knew who the best player was at offensive tackle.

Now, translate that to college coaching and Alabama. What if an assistant coach leaves? Well, it's easy. A new coach takes over a particular recruiting area, and the standards for the program, position by position, are the same. That new coach has to follow the system's grading scale, just as did the previous coach. He has to ask the exact same questions about a player's "critical factors."

"In Nick's system, it doesn't matter who the coach is in that area," Lombardi said.

What the caretakers of the Browns developed—and what Saban paid close attention to and had input with—was a system that uniformly described and defined every player on the field so the player could accurately be graded. For instance, Cleveland defensive ends were to be 6-foot-4 and weigh 270 pounds and run a 5.0-second 40-yard dash. Then the critical factors came into play and players were graded on those. For all players (except quarterbacks and kickers) critical factors included among other things:

- athletic ability, which was quickness, agility, balance
- strength/explosion
- playing speed—the ability to run fast with pads on
- competitiveness, which was toughness and intensity
- size/arm length
- character

"The easiest way to explain it is, we had an overlay of what we wanted in a player for each position," Lombardi said. "When we laid it over a player we were scouting, and if it matched, we went for the player. We would have to change definitions and fine-tune so it was an ongoing process to be right with the definition of each position. It was a collaborative effort.

"We went down to Dallas when Nick was on the Cleveland staff, and the Cowboys had linebackers that were so much faster than ours. We knew we had to modify the system because we had too many big linebackers that were slow. It was an ever-changing process. We were trying to chase perfection in our definitions of players position by position."

In the Browns' system a player with superior athletic ability in the critical factors of athletic ability, strength/explosion, playing speed, competitiveness, and size was given a 7. He was given a 4 if he was inconsistent, or a 3 if he had low athletic ability, which eliminated him from the draft. The system was blunt. It said the heck with players who didn't show up with God's gifts of speed and height.

The Browns were looking for players with final averages of 6.5–8.0, which meant the player would project as a starter. The grades 6.0–6.4 meant possible starter. If 5.7–5.9, he was classified as "make it," or fifth to eighth round. Savage said the only player he ever graded at 8.0 was the Michigan defensive back and Heisman Trophy winner, Charles Woodson, who has had an All-Pro career.

The Browns would also put letters or tags next to a player's name on the draft board. *B* if he lacked bulk. *Z* if he lacked verifiable height. *C* was for character issues. The Browns wanted "clean" players, ones who did not get their number downgraded by having letters all over their name on the board. With a letter next to your name, your highest possible grade was 6.4, which was still a possible starter. It was a stringent system.

"The objective in the building," Lombardi said, "was to acquire players with no letters. If you didn't take a player because of a letter and they went ahead and made it in the NFL, God bless them, they beat the percentages."

What these definitions and grades did for the NFL team was eliminate players from consideration for the draft. For Alabama, the system pares down the list of possible recruits. Bama starts with a list of seven hundred to eight hundred names for each recruiting class, then starts to whittle. The height, weight, and speed parameters allow Alabama to focus on a manageable number of players who fit the Bama system. The Crimson Tide is big on prototypes for each position and does not often stray from them.

"What the system does is, it requires you to define a position," Lombardi said. "When Bill came in to Cleveland, he gave us a definition of what he wanted the team to be, what his vision of the team was. It is the same thing with Alabama. Nick's vision translated into the grading system, and that translates into the players. You scout inside out, not outside in. You scout for players that fit what you do inside your building as opposed to looking for players here and there. You define what you want, and when the player fits the criteria, you're interested. If he doesn't meet the criteria, you're not interested.

"Nick didn't just wake up and say, 'Hey, give me the top twenty-five recruits.' "

In essence, what Saban did at LSU and what he is doing at Alabama is not about collecting talent. Not even close. He is building a team. He does not start with players, he starts with definitions of players, just as the Cowboys and the Browns did. When Alabama goes recruiting, it is not finding players, it is eliminating players because it has defined what it wants at each position. If you are not this height and weight with this speed and you do not reach certain benchmarks in the critical factors for the position, the Crimson Tide drops you off the list.

Here is how it starts. Alabama collects sales leads. It pores over newspaper clippings and Internet message boards. It jots down names, perhaps a tip that came from the uncle of the woman who works in the mail room. You know that tip: "Bama ought to look at this kid from Huntsville" or some other town.

Alabama also tracks Twitter and follows the recruiting mavens who go to the Nike camps and Under Armour Combines, where coaches are not allowed. The Tide's recruiting staff looks over the e-mails that come in with leads about the spectacular eighth-grade or freshman player.

At the start, Alabama does not care if the reporting from this array of sources is 100 percent credible. In time, the coaches and personnel staff will determine if it is. What they are doing is compiling an early catalog of names, preferably within that golden recruiting area of a five-hour drive in any direction from campus.

When the names are assembled for a particular recruiting class, the real work begins. The first thing is to get players on campus for summer camps and put them through Alabama's drills. Saban has to see them. The youth camps, ages seven to twelve, can average fourteen hundred campers. The more important camps, freshmen through rising seniors, draw six hundred per session. An offensive-line/defensive-line camp draws another four hundred, plus a two-day 7-on-7 camp brings in thirty to forty teams.

Because of these camps and all the film that Alabama coaches gather, they do not buy into hype, which comes at the Bama recruiters from every angle. They scout with their eyes, not their ears. People are trying to influence Alabama coaches every day about a player, but the system pushes away "the friend of the program" trying to advocate for a player. If players do not fit into the system with height-weight-speed and critical factors for their position, they are discarded. That's how Alabama assistant coaches can turn off all the chatter and glide through all the text messages they get about various high school players.

"If you don't have an anchor system, you can get caught up in the fog of confusion in scouting college players and recruiting high school players," Savage said.

There is no fog with exact definitions of players. Outside linebackers in Alabama's 3-4 need to be at least 6-foot-3½, 240 to 250 pounds, with long arms so they can reach the offensive tackle first with their hands and then beat him on the edge. Adrian Hubbard, a redshirt sophomore, is the prototype at 6-foot-6, 248 pounds, because he can engage blockers before they engage him. The Bama inside linebackers have to project to 260 pounds, which is defensive-line size for other schools, but the Tide wants those inside backers to take on guards all day.

Alabama does not like little people. It likes big people. Heavyweights do not fight lightweights for a reason: big people beat up little people. The Crimson Tide, more than anything else, is about big, physical players. Bama is built for power and explosive playmakers.

You might look at the Tide's Dee Hart, the 5-foot-9, 180-pound back, as an outlier, but the system has room for "specialty" players, those kids who can fly and return kicks and be a third-down back. It's not all thumpers.

Just look at the Alabama corners. They have to be at least 5-foot-11 and able to tackle. If they can't tackle, forget it, Alabama walks away without thinking twice. If corners can't tackle, the Tide cannot have a balanced defense.

Alabama takes an NFL approach to personnel. It ranks players on a board, much like the NFL. It sets its board and does not care what other people think. In fact, when Alabama offers a player, that player has been known to receive multiple offers within two weeks, perhaps as many as twenty-five.

Alabama has a general disdain for the five-star, four-star, any star, rankings of high school players. In the Cleveland system, they do not want scouts to say, "This is a third-rounder." In the Bama system they do not want coaches to say, "This is a four-star." Alabama feels that system is flawed, not just because as many two-star players as five-star players make it as starters in the NFL, but also because Bama is recruiting to its definitions. It does not care what the recruiting mavens think, or what the recruiters of other schools think.

"The system allows scouts and recruiters to see players through the same lens," Savage said. "You take the emotions out of it and evaluate in a systematic way. It pulls everyone together so they are looking at the same thing."

Tennessee has had three coaches in five years, and a hodgepodge of players are now in Knoxville. It happens in pro ball, too, and it helps explain the Vols' losing records the last two years. There has been no uniformity.

Other programs, those outside the SEC, see a big guy with athletic ability and think wideout. Saban thinks defense. Alabama sees a bigger body on a lean frame with speed and is thinking shutdown corner. Always, the Alabama head coach sees players from a defensive perspective. Look at Mark Barron, a sensational offensive player in high school. He was a safety at Alabama and became a first-round NFL pick in 2012.

Mike Clayton, the former LSU wide receiver, saw Saban evaluate players in Baton Rouge and move them around and then watched them succeed. Corey Webster was a receiver and became a very rich defensive back in the NFL. Marcus Spears was a tight end and became a wealthy defensive end in the NFL. Joseph Addai was a quarterback and became a rich running back in the NFL.

"Saban came from the NFL and he knows what an NFL coach is looking for," Clayton said. "If you have size and good feet, if you are good enough in my eyes to play this one position in college, he says, you are good enough to play it in the NFL, where the money is.

"No player at the time wanted to do what he said, at first. They all thought he was out to get them. They were upset, they scored touchdowns in high school, they wanted to be in the limelight. He switched them over to defense and he required them to be great. He instilled confidence in them; they had to compete to be great, and he would coach them harder, and he made them into good players. I saw it with my own two eyes."

Alabama rates players on a scale from 1 to 5, with 5 being limited and 1 being rare. The Crimson Tide does not recruit 5s and it hunts for 1s. They settle for those players who are 2.2 on the scale.

"The player will grade himself if you watch enough film," Savage said.

It helps that Alabama can start with the specimens, the high school kids who are already big and fast. When you win national championships you can attract those kinds of players. Still, Saban has every recruit meet with the strength and conditioning coach Scott Cochran to evaluate the player's frame and growth potential. If there is an issue, the player is marked on the recruiting board with a tag or an alert. In Cleveland it was simply a *B* for lacks bulk or *Z* for lacks height, among other alerts.

Alabama is more cautious about putting alerts or tags on players because it starts researching these players when they are fifteen and sixteen years old. The Tide coaches have to see the player in person and then put him in the hopper for further evaluation. The staff is conscious of a young player's frame and whether he has the wide shoulders and the look of a player who can add bulk. If they pass that look, then Alabama starts to get position-specific and study critical factors such as the ability to bend, overall athletic ability, and strength/explosion.

Believe it or not, Alabama was not on to Trent Richardson at the start of his junior season in Pensacola, Florida. He had an ankle injury and there was no way to project him forward. Richardson healed and signed with Alabama over Florida, probably thanks to a boost from an administrator at his school who once worked for the Alabama athletic department. He was a first-round draft pick of the NFL in 2012.

Alabama digs in when it recruits players and investigates whether the players can take hard coaching. Alabama is a difficult place to play, and mental makeup is an important factor, a critical factor, in recruiting a player.

Alabama will put a neon-yellow dot next to a recruit who has academic issues. An orange dot goes next to players who have character issues. These players need to be investigated more. Was there a criminal act? Is the player coachable? The character dots came from Marciniak, who worked for Tom Landry and Gil Brandt of the Cowboys. He would place a black dot next to a player with character issues, criminal acts, etc., and the Cowboys were not likely to draft that player. Marciniak said he didn't get to put many of those black dots on the draft board, so he had to be right.

If the measurables of height, weight, speed, are not there, Alabama is not interested in a player. If an assistant still swears by a high school player, he has to go through Saban to get a name on the big board, which is not easy. The head coach has the final authority, much as Belichick had the final say on the board with the Browns. The Alabama staff has no independent contractors standing up in meetings and declaring a player ready to go for a scholarship. The vetting of a player always ends with the general manager, who is also the head coach, and that is Nick Saban.

"Nick said one time that in pro football you get one pick every thirty-two choices," Savage said, "but in college, he said, if we are picking the right guys, we could be signing four or five first-rounders every year."

In the 2010 draft, two Alabama players (linebacker Rolando McClain, Oakland; and cornerback Kareem Jackson, Houston) were picked in the first round. In the 2011 draft, four Alabama players (defensive lineman Marcell Dareus, Buffalo; wide receiver Julio Jones, Atlanta; offensive lineman James Carpenter, Seattle; running back Mark Ingram, New Orleans) were picked in the first round. In the 2012 draft, four Alabama players (running back Trent Richardson, Cleveland; safety Mark Barron, Tampa Bay; cornerback Dre Kirkpatrick, Bengals; linebacker Dont'a Hightower, Patriots) were taken in the first round. A near miss on a fifth first-rounder was linebacker Courtney Upshaw, the first pick of the second round by Baltimore.

The 2008 recruiting class actually produced five first-round picks. Because of injuries, Hightower and Barron actually came out a year later than projected. The 2009 class had three when you include tackle James Carpenter with Richardson and Kirkpatrick.

One Alabama insider said it is the job of the assistant coach to persuade Saban on a player, which means acquiring more information, investigating deeper, and making sure the player has been to camp. Saban puts in the work watching film of players. He knows whom he likes and doesn't like. The people who have worked for Saban find it hard to believe any other college head coach puts more effort into recruiting.

It is not easy for Saban's assistant coaches to disagree with the boss on a player. "I have learned working with Nick," said Tommy Moffitt, the LSU strength coach, "that if he likes a guy, you better keep your mouth shut."

The Alabama strongman has legitimately been rapped for the oversigning of players and NFL-style roster management. Saban has also been censured by media for Alabama's use of medical redshirts. The *Wall Street Journal* reported that players who were not really hurt were forced off the scholarship roll under the guise of being injured because Alabama wanted to use the scholarship for a better player. But on several occasions Saban has dismissed players from the team and pushed for them to take medical redshirts because they failed multiple drug tests. He didn't want the bus to roll over a kid twice: once for the drug bust, a second time with a smear to the kid's reputation if the news of a positive drug test got out. The designation as a "medical redshirt" brought fewer questions as to why a player was no longer with the program, with less chance his reputation would be harmed.

A potential issue with Alabama players who make it through one of the most rigorous programs in all of college football is, can an NFL team get more out of the player than Saban did? Think about it. The Alabama player is inside an NFL system for three or four years and climbing toward a peak. He has been coached by an NFL-caliber coach. Does he hit a ceiling in Tuscaloosa? We'll find out with this run of players such as Mark Ingram, Julio Jones, Rolando McClain, among others. I'm just asking. I don't know.

What Alabama is running into in recruiting these days is the rival school telling the recruit, "They have too many guys at that position, great players, you shouldn't go there." The Tide turns it around on the rival school by telling the high school recruit, "They must not think much of you; we think you can play here and you will be just fine."

The players who come on campus for the ninth-to-twelfth-grade camps have notes put in their files constantly. They are measured, and if they do not project to reach the definitions for a position, they are dropped off the list one by one. It is not easy work. The Alabama class of 2014 still had four hundred names on it in April 2012. When the Tide first started to investigate players for the 2014 class, it had seven hundred to eight hundred names.

The Crimson Tide will eventually offer one hundred scholarships to those four hundred, which absolutely blows away Steve Spurrier's contention that Saban has only to snap his fingers for recruits to sign for Alabama. The South Carolina coach said:

"He's got a nice little gig going, a little bit like [John] Calipari. He tells guys, 'Hey, three years from now, you're going to be a first-round pick and go.' If he wants to be the greatest coach or one of the greatest coaches in college football, to me, he has to go somewhere besides Alabama and win, because they've always won there at Alabama."

Saban does have a nice gig. Rabid fans, big stadium, a lot of cash, and on and on. But Spurrier should look at page 194 of the 2011 Alabama media guide. From 2003 to 2006, the four years under Coach Mike Shula, the Crimson Tide was 26-24. Spurrier then has to look at page 193. In four years under coach Mike DuBose (1997 to 2000), Alabama was 24-23.

You do not just toss the footballs out on the field and win at Alabama. It takes recruiting and coaching. The quick fact check suggests that Spurrier poked at Bama without a lot of thought, or maybe he was just bored and wanted to pick on somebody the way he used to do when he had great teams at Florida (he has a great team percolating at South Carolina).

Perhaps Spurrier should have said, "They've always won there at Alabama . . . when they have had the right coach."

Bear Bryant was the right coach. Gene Stallings was the right coach. Nick Saban is the right coach.

The Crimson Tide went from 1978 to 1992 without a national championship. Spurrier made it sound as if titles fall off the trees for Alabama. Here is the thing to remember about Alabama's being all-powerful. The Crimson Tide cannot simply wave a scholarship in front of a high school player. Other schools, other coaches, are bearing down in recruiting, too. If Alabama offers a player, it is likely that player has a desk drawer full of offers. Remember, the Tide is offering one hundred, not twenty-five. It shares the boat on a player with other schools, whether media or rival coaches believe it or not. Bama gets turned down.

Throughout the recruiting of a player Saban has given a mandate: "Do not compromise the process." It's what the Browns preached and what the Cowboys preached before that.

Savage, who was a scout for the Browns and later the general manager, said the system gave Saban a foundation, a root system, on how to evaluate players, which he took to Michigan State, then LSU, then the Dolphins, and finally Alabama.

The system has wheels, that's for sure. Savage was the scouting director for the Baltimore Ravens when the Ravens were building their Super Bowl championship team, and he used the system with general manager Ozzie Newsome, who also had worked for the Browns. Savage took the system with him to Cleveland when he became general manager. Variations and disciples of the system are spread throughout the NFL.

Saban, according to NFL personnel men and scouts that know him, has a vast mental library on players. That is, he can look at a player, then search back through his mind and say, "He reminds me of that player, and he will project into this kind of player." This is not judging snowflakes, where no two are alike. Some football players are similar to other football players. If you are a coach or a scout and can recall a player of similar talent, it is a significant advantage in scouting, or, in the case of a college coach, recruiting. This comparison shopping is invaluable.

That library may be how the Crimson Tide hit it big with an outlier to the system—Courtney Upshaw. Upshaw was an outlier no matter what the recruiting services said. He had shorter arms, his weight was in between that of a linebacker and a defensive lineman, and he did not play in a football hotbed. According to people familiar with Alabama's recruiting class of 2008, Upshaw was rated in the middle of the class, even though he was rated as one of the top prospects in the South by recruiting services. What position was he going to play at Alabama? There was no precise definition of Upshaw's ability.

Here is where Saban's library must have come into play. Somewhere in his years in football he had seen a player like Upshaw on film or on the field, and Upshaw reminded Saban of the player, or the coach's instincts kicked in. Upshaw was an outlier to the Browns/Cowboys/Alabama system, but Alabama offered him a scholarship anyway. Maybe it was because he was an in-state kid and Bama had to offer him, or maybe the Tide needed an extra linebacker that year. As it turned out, Upshaw had a terrific college career. He was a marauder off the edge and shed blockers with powerful hands and was as competitive as any player on the roster.

Upshaw took in all the coaching from linebackers coach Sal Sunseri, working constantly on hand placement, exploding up through his body into opponents, committed to getting better. Alabama insiders will tell you that Sunseri's best work in Tuscaloosa was with Upshaw, who became a technician. Sunseri is now the defensive coordinator at Tennessee.

The same concerns about height, weight, and speed that followed Upshaw into college followed him into the 2012 draft. In January 2012, he was projected by some as a top fifteen pick; then he started to slide as his measurables were studied. Still, he was a Saban guy, which counts for something with NFL personnel men. What's more, Upshaw was productive for a national championship team. Upshaw wasn't likely to slide far because of his Alabama pedigree, and he didn't. He was the first pick of the second round by Baltimore, whose general manager is Ozzie Newsome, the former Alabama all-American, who took the scouting system from Cleveland to Baltimore and won a Super Bowl.

An even better example of an outlier is Ray Lewis, the All-Pro linebacker for the Ravens. Lewis had tags as a college player at Miami. There was a Z because he wasn't quite tall enough for the position. Other linebackers were rated ahead of him. He's still playing in the NFL and is headed to the NFL Hall of Fame.

Saban is perfect for the system because he is deliberate and because of his discipline. He will not stray from it; he demands some order. Marciniak saw the discipline in the Browns' defensive backs in July 1991 during training camp when Saban was defensive coordinator, and also in charge of defensive backs. When the rest of the team came out for practice, shirttails were out, loose bits of tape dangled from arms, shirts might have been cut off, and because it was training camp, players stopped to chat with fans. When the defensive backs came out on the field, they marched right to their appointed spot on the field, with Saban waiting for them. Their shirts were tucked in, socks were the same color, and nothing about them was scraggly. In training camp they did not sign autographs on the way to the field as players at other positions might. They got to work.

"It was that way right at the start of camp when he might have twenty guys in his group with some of them certain to be cut," Marciniak said. "It might have been the only discipline they had gotten in their lives. That was the line you had to toe if you wanted to play defensive back for the Cleveland Browns. It was that way for veterans and rookies.

"I just kept thinking to myself, 'How can one man make a big group of twenty guys behave like that?' He and I are not real good friends. I'm telling you this out of respect."

Saban demanded that rookies handle drills the same way the veterans handled drills. The expectations were always high, Marciniak said. When the defensive backs left the Browns' meeting room, chairs were always in a row, trash picked up and put away. And never, ever could they be late.

"The expression he always used with a player: 'Don't give me any bull****.' They knew," Marciniak said. "He was young, but dominant. It all carries over from the practice field to the game."

It's been twenty years since Marciniak watched Saban whip his DBs into shape. Still, when he sees an NFL defensive back act up on the field, Marciniak will turn to his wife, Delores, and say, "He wouldn't be doing that stuff with Nick Saban around."

Dom Anile, who was the college scouting director for the Browns, would not let Saban get away with being all-business. He would pass the Browns coach in the hallway, and Saban was usually walking with his head down. Anile would bark at Saban, "Hey, Nick, it's not game day. Smile."

Saban would flash a smile, put his head down, and walk on.

"People would ask me, 'Who is this grumpy guy Saban?' And I would say, 'He's not grumpy, not all the time,' " Anile said. "He is a really funny guy.

"We used to take Art Modell's Learjet all over the place to work out players, and Nick would be on the field working the players out and drawing a sweat. He would yell over at me, 'You're the director of personnel. How come you're standing around at these workouts like you are the head coach and I'm doing all the work?'

"Nick had a sense of humor. He really did. He used to throw a good party, too. I remember one that was during the Kentucky Derby. He could play cards, too. I'm telling you, people got him all wrong. He wasn't a drinker, but he was cordial and would have a beer with you."

Tom Lemming, the recruiting analyst, said Saban will not hire buddies for assistant coaching jobs. He wants coaches who are good recruiters and good coaches. "I don't think Nick Saban plays golf," Lemming said. "I think his hobby is recruiting. There is nobody like him, except for Urban Meyer."

Saban is not immune to the mistake. Alabama has missed on some players because they did not get the player to camp or the player rushed the Tide into a decision on whether to offer him, which doesn't happen often. Saban also missed on a player when he called one of his players on the LSU roster "dumb." The Mobile player LSU was recruiting refused LSU's offer because of the comment. The recruit's father said, "Maybe he was going to call my son dumb." Mostly, though, Saban does not make mistakes. He will not exaggerate anything to a family during recruiting, said Lemming. He lays out what the university can do for the player academically, and what the program can do for them athletically.

When a mistake is made and a player does not achieve, Alabama does not move on without a look back. The Crimson Tide reevaluates the player and tries to understand why the mistake was made and how to prevent its happening again. Alabama will study the player and add to its library of knowledge of what went wrong.

Alabama can recruit all the right players and still get knocked down unexpectedly. The Crimson Tide was 12-0 in 2008, then lost to eventual national champion Florida in the SEC Championship Game, then was stunned by Utah in the Sugar Bowl. In the run-up to the Sugar Bowl game, the Utes felt disrespected by Alabama, so when the captains for the two teams stood at midfield for the coin toss, Utah linebacker Stevenson Sylvester looked across at the Bama players and said, "We're going to kick your ass."

Archie Manning, one of the honorary captains of that seventy-fifth Sugar Bowl, and a New Orleans resident, had told friends the Utes didn't have a chance against an SEC team such as Alabama. After the coin toss, Manning went over to Kevin Plank, the CEO of Under Armour and the equipment provider for Utah, and said, "I've changed my mind."

Utah won, 31–17. The Tide faithful blamed it on the loss of all-American tackle Andre Smith, whom Saban suspended for involvement with an agent. Alabama also lost offensive lineman Mike Johnson to an injury during the game. More of a problem for the Crimson Tide was the inability of their corners to deal with Utah's short passing game and the Utes' tall wideouts, which is rarely an issue any longer for Alabama defensive backs.

That Utah game was two seasons into the "system" at Alabama. For the most part, Alabama does not get surprised anymore. Saban's record is 50-12 going into the 2012 season (five wins were vacated because of an NCAA violation). His big people beat up other programs' people, big or little, and he has two SEC championships and two national championships to show for it at Alabama.

The system worked at LSU and at Alabama, and Lombardi said it would have worked with the Miami Dolphins, where Saban coached in 2005 and 2006. "When you run this system, you have to have everybody buy into the system, and the Dolphins did not have everybody buy in," Lombardi said.

Alabama has a head coach who has had fourteen jobs in football. Saban is past sixty years old. He has a vast mental library of knowledge of players, and he knows how to coach up players and develop them. He does four jobs for his $5.9 million a year, and as difficult as it might be for some to believe, he earns his money as head coach, defensive backs coach, general manager, and fund-raiser. He earns every nickel.

"The Nick Saban that Alabama has gotten is the culmination of what a head coach is supposed to be," Savage said. "He has, through trial and error, figured out what works and what doesn't work, and all the different aspects of running the game on the field, to the strength and conditioning and weight room and off-season program, to the recruiting philosophy and approach, dealing with alums, and dealing with media.

"He has mastered all of them and put them into action at Alabama."

CHAPTER 12

The night before Arkansas played Ohio State in the Sugar Bowl in New Orleans at the end of the 2010 season, a crowd gathered in the middle of Bourbon Street. A fan of the Razorbacks and a fan of the Buckeyes, each fueled by the customary mix of alcohol and school pride, were throwing fists at one another.

"It was like a cage match," said Ron Higgins, a reporter for the *Memphis Commercial Appeal*.

When the Arkansas fan started to land a series of blows and finally wore out the Ohio State fan, the crowd did not yell, "Woo Pig Sooie," the call of the Hogs.

It started chanting, "SEC, SEC, SEC," in a salute to the Arkansas brawler, as if he were carrying the banner of the Southeastern Conference with those closed fists.

No matter what the occasion, these SEC folks have to be in the front seat, the first in line, the quickest to the door, on top of the pile—win the fight. The chant "SEC, SEC, SEC"—we're first, you're not—has been a familiar refrain the last six years. Alabama won titles in 2009 and 2011. Florida claimed the crowns in 2006 and 2008. Auburn won in 2010 and LSU in 2007.

No wonder the rest of college football appeared to be using the coming four-team play-off as an instrument to silence those SEC chanters. When it was proposed that conference champions be admitted "only" to the four-team play-off, there was instant paranoia in the South. SEC fans saw a conspiracy; but who can blame the rest of the BCS if they considered for a moment how to keep the SEC at bay with some politics to avoid another all-SEC National Championship Game, which is what happened in 2011.

At some point, politics will give way to football, and somebody is going to have to beat the SEC on the field. The list of contenders from other conferences starts with Southern Cal and Oregon of the Pac-12, Michigan State of the Big Ten, and Florida State of the ACC. Texas, even with all its loot, is not getting much attention, and Ohio State has to wait out a postseason ban.

But never mind who's next for the other leagues. Who's Next for the SEC?

I have a program in mind.

Georgia.

Here's the background.

In December 2009, head coach Mark Richt went looking for a defensive coordinator, and the Bulldogs started their search at the top with the big-name candidates. Then the Dawgs proceeded to land . . . with a thud.

No thanks, said Kirby Smart, the Alabama defensive coordinator, whose team was about to win the national championship. Why should he make a move to Georgia, his alma mater, and become defensive coordinator when Smart might have a chance to become the Bulldogs' head coach in a few years? You can imagine the conversation between Smart and his boss, the Alabama head coach, Nick Saban, who told Smart to sit tight and wait perhaps for the Georgia coaching job to come open. By the way, here is a pay raise, Kirby, to more than double the $360,000 pittance that you were making.

No thanks, said candidate No. 2, Bud Foster, the Virginia Tech defensive coordinator. But thank you for reaching out. Foster makes just $432,660, but after some overtures from other schools, Foster signed a deal in January 2010 for a reported annuity of $800,000 if he stayed at Tech through the 2014 season.

No thanks, said John Chavis, who stayed at LSU and will be knocking down a million a year as his deal matures.

Its rivals were gleeful that Georgia swung and missed, and swung and missed, and swung a third time and missed again. That was three strikes, but the Bulldogs did not strike out. Not even close. Georgia has a lot to sell. They have an even-tempered head coach who knows football, a huge stadium, facilities, money, the allegiance of an entire state, and a wealth of talented high school players to pick from. Considering the number of high school players the state produces, Georgia has as many resources to build a national champion as Alabama, LSU, and Florida.

So Georgia swung again—a fourth time—and this time it found its guy, Todd Grantham, an NFL coach, who was hired January 15, 2010. He was actually the best man for the job all along. Indeed, Grantham was invented just for this job. Georgia finished fifth nationally in total defense in 2011, but that's not all that makes Grantham a transformer for the program. It's the culture he brings to the defense, that big people beat up little people. He also brings elements of the Cleveland Browns/Alabama scouting/recruiting formula, the 3-4 defense, the reliance on the defensive front 7, and a little attitude.

The SEC in the last six years has become a collection of programs trying to become the NFL's thirty-third franchise. Schools have hired player personnel directors and have adopted NFL-style recruiting philosophies. They have declared that the way to win football games is from the inside out, tackle to tackle, big people beating up little people. They want to have multiple running backs in the stable and get as many big backs as they can, preferably in the range of 215 to 220 pounds. Programs have hired coaches with NFL experience—Brian VanGorder and Scot Loeffler joined Auburn in 2012—and stuff their media guides with pictures of their former players in the NFL. They have put their best athletes on defense, not offense, and have gone hard into the junior college ranks to find defensive linemen, the players that truly separate the SEC from the rest of college football.

And here comes Grantham, who worked in the NFL for the Dallas Cowboys, Houston Texans, Cleveland Browns, and Indianapolis Colts and worked for Nick Saban at Michigan State and discusses football with Bill Belichick, the New England Patriots head coach. Grantham works in the SEC, but NFL is all over his résumé. He likes big people on defense, just like the coach at Alabama he used to work for. Grantham is ambitious and covets run stoppers, and he uses the Cleveland Browns–inspired player-evaluation scheme when he recruits for Georgia's defense.

Now scan the Georgia recruiting class of 2011. What do you see among the defensive guys? Big people. Georgia did not sign anyone for defense in 2011 who it measured at less than six feet tall, Grantham said. That was his first recruiting cycle. The Bulldogs dueled Alabama for those thumpers at linebacker that could fly inside Georgia's 3-4 defense, which is also the scheme the Crimson Tide runs.

Do you sign off on all defensive recruits? Grantham was asked. "Yes," he said. He knows what he wants.

Look at Malcolm Mitchell, who was forced to be a receiver in 2011 because Georgia needed some depth at receiver. Grantham helped recruit Mitchell, who is 6-foot-1, as a cornerback. He is an athlete, and Grantham insists Mitchell will play defense 100 percent of the time in 2012. The ideal corner is 5-foot-11 and well built. Mitchell will do just fine, even if he is a couple of inches taller, because he can flip those hips, turn and run, and stay between receivers and the ball or close on the ball fast enough to make plays.

Now look at the rest of the defense with linebacker Jarvis Jones and linebacker Alec Ogletree and nose tackle Jonathan Jenkins. There is also a 6-foot-2 corner in Sanders Commings. Georgia had nine starters back on defense to start the 2012 season. Many of them were in Athens before Grantham showed up, but he and the other Georgia assistants, as well as head coach Richt, are adding depth and creeping up the talent scale on the defensive side of the ball. Look out for the linebacker Ray Drew and 6-foot-1 defensive back Damian Swann. NFL scouts have said the last several seasons that Georgia's issue on defense was size. The players were not as good as advertised because they were not big enough. If you don't believe it, just look at the Bulldogs in the past drafts. See any first-round picks lately on defense? Size is not an issue for 2012.

The Bulldogs had one of the best quarterbacks in the SEC in Aaron Murray to start the 2012 season, and they had reliable running backs again, nearly a fleet of them like LSU and Alabama. We're not sure about the quality of the offensive line, but at least a former Alabama guy, assistant coach Will Friend, is in charge of the unit, and he believes the physical culture of a football team starts with the offensive line.

But back to defense, which wins championships. What Georgia needs on defense is not Bulldogs, it needs hellhounds, fliers with size and ill disposition, again like Alabama and LSU. Jesse Williams, the Alabama defensive end, now the 2012 Bama nose tackle, said the Crimson Tide defense went into the 2011 season an agitated group that wanted to embarrass offenses and shove them into a phone booth and play intimidating football. That's what Georgia needs to do to resurrect itself and be Next in the SEC. The defense, along with a favorable 2012 schedule, set up the Bulldogs for a big season in 2012.

Grantham is just the badass to spark something bigger than an appearance in the SEC Championship Game. He got into a post-game skirmish with the Vanderbilt head coach James Franklin and flashed a choke sign at the Florida placekicker Chas Henry. He can have a crusty edge to him, which is just what Georgia fans think Richt lacks. This guy Grantham ought to satisfy the unreasonable Bulldogs fans who think Richt doesn't bark enough. More than anything, Grantham knows the 3-4 and its multiple looks and versatility in blitzes with those outside backers. With veteran starters, the Bulldogs should be back in the top five in total defense in 2012.

Georgia has not had a defensive player taken in the first round of the NFL since 2005. It will have at least one in 2013 (Jones) and could have three more in the early rounds (Ogletree, Jenkins, and nose guard Kwame Geathers). Georgia is not the Crimson Tide on defense, but the Bulldogs have made strides. SEC schools are accustomed to having draft picks, but if they are in the bottom half of the draft, that makes for only a good team, not a great team. Georgia again has players on defense who will ascend to the top half of the draft. These players have freakish athletic ability, touched on the way out, as they say, but they have to be schooled by good coaching.

Georgia is offering some schooling, along with some attitude from its defensive coordinator.

A few other factors make Georgia a prime candidate to join the SEC parade of champions in the next several seasons.

The school completed a $40 million expansion to its football facilities in 2011. The Bulldogs, who have not been a serious national contender for five years, now have a gleaming, polished football complex and renewed vigor in recruiting. Georgia wanted to compete again on the same playing field as the national contenders in the SEC, and here was a new spark in facilities, the *Wow!* factor. Recruits get that.

Here is another signpost. The former Georgia star Hines Ward told the *Atlanta Journal-Constitution* that for the Bulldogs to be a national championship contender again, they had to trap the best players in their state and not let them flee to Bama or LSU or Florida. It is how Saban put LSU back on the rails starting with the 2001 recruiting class. He built a fence to keep them in and a fence to keep others out. If Georgia erects a taller fence to keep in its best players, it will without question be a steady top ten program and national contender. The state is overrun with quality players. The top two senior prospects in the nation in 2012 are from Georgia. In June 2011, one hundred rising senior high school football players in the state had already been offered Division I football scholarships, according to Michael Carvell of the *Atlanta Journal-Constitution*. Alabama had thirteen players from Georgia on its 2011 roster. Ward, a star with Super Bowl rings, sounded as if he wanted to grab on to the Bulldogs wave and help close the borders to the Tide. What will help more is if Georgia wins big in 2012 and 2013 and the state's best high school players find their way to Athens more often.

Then there is Richt, who has been in Athens eleven seasons. His record is 106-38, which is the fourth-best mark (.741) among active coaches. He remade his strength and conditioning program after some late-game losses in 2010. LSU, Alabama, and Florida have demonstrated with multiple championships since 2003 that muscle rules in the SEC, and strength and conditioning is never to be taken lightly. Speed is significant, but size and speed is more significant. Richt seems to have adjusted his view of the world when it comes to getting those big, fast people.

What's curious is that Richt was the longest-tenured coach in the SEC going into the 2012 season (eleven seasons), but sixth in salary at $2.8 million. His incentives with the new deal he signed are significant ($800,000 for a national championship), yet he is still not a $3-million-a-year coach. Perhaps it is the hometown discount because Richt has said UGA is his last coaching job. Perhaps Georgia is holding back the $3 mil until there is a national championship.

The next two seasons could be Georgia's window, but honestly, there should be a window each season with what Georgia has to offer. Only the Gators have a deeper talent base in their state, but they have to share it with Miami and Florida State. Georgia has to share its talent with Georgia Tech, but even then Tech's admission requirements allegedly prevent them from recruiting some of the same players as UGA. Georgia, bigger in population than Louisiana, has more players to choose from than LSU.

———

So who's Next if Georgia does not take advantage of its talent and favorable schedule? Well, it was Arkansas, before Coach Bobby Petrino was caught with a mistress and fired. The Razorbacks will be plenty formidable in 2012 and play LSU and Alabama at home, so it sets up as a nice season. Still, it won't be quite the same mesh with John L. Smith as the coach. It's not his team.

So, if you had to pick Next after Georgia as the SEC team to challenge for a national title, it would be South Carolina. Steve Spurrier was supposed to have revolutionized football in the SEC twenty years ago with his Fun N Gun offense, but now the Ball Coach is right in step with the old ways of the conference. He has a 220-pound tailback and a good defense. The Gamecocks run the ball and stop the run. If you were paying attention in 2011, LSU and Alabama had the same formula while finishing 1-2 nationally in the regular season.

South Carolina was viewed as a less than desirable job before Spurrier got there in 2005, but the day he retires, Carolina can go out and talk to most coaches in the business and have them look twice at accepting the position. The state is teeming with talent because it has attracted new business, which means more families and more recruits. The school has some of the most faithful fans in college football, and they are going to be rewarded in 2012 and 2013.

Spurrier is still one of the best coaches in all of college football, a Hall of Famer, and he will have superstars on both sides of the ball in 2012. Running back Marcus Lattimore is returning from a knee injury, and defensive end Jadeveon Clowney is going to demand a lot of attention from blockers, and those kinds of guys make the whole unit better. The Gamecocks were 8-0 against Georgia, Tennessee, Florida, and Clemson in 2010 and 2011 and will be a certifiable top ten or top fifteen team.

What about Auburn, the 2010 national champion? Are they not still in the mix? No, not until Brian VanGorder gets the defense straightened out. The Tigers have the fourth-best talent in the SEC West.

"When you say Next, what I think about is Auburn realizing that Cam Newton was a lightning-in-a-bottle situation, and now they are going to a more pro-style system to try and negate what Alabama and LSU have done in the NFL draft," said Phil Savage, the Senior Bowl executive director, former general manager of the Cleveland Browns, and college scout and assistant coach.

"When I think Next, it is which coach that has come out of the Saban tree is going to put it together and find their footing for their school. Derek Dooley at Tennessee? Will Muschamp at Florida? Will it be Jimbo Fisher at Florida State with what he does in the ACC? Is it any of them? Is it none of them? That's Next for me."

Things have become so competitive in the SEC that Dooley has overhauled most of his staff in just two seasons and snatched a coach from his old boss Saban. Tennessee hired Bama linebackers coach Sal Sunseri to run the Vols' defense after failing to lure LSU's John Chavis back to Knoxville with a million bucks. Dooley became the UT head coach in 2010, and seven assistant coaches, plus the strength and conditioning coach, have already departed following seasons of 6-7 and 5-7 (4-12 in SEC games).

"Is it normal to have seven coaches transition in a year? No, it's very rare for something like that to happen," Dooley said during an interview with the *Chattanooga Times Free Press*. "But I kind of view it as sort of a correction. When you start a company, when you start anything, you always have that little initial correction to kind of fix all the things maybe you didn't get right in the beginning."

The next correction in the hypercompetitive SEC is for Dooley to be shown the door.

And what of LSU, which has won 24 games the last two seasons, but not a national championship? What's next about the Tigers?

"I think we're about to throw the ball better than we have in years," LSU coach Les Miles said in May 2012. "The guy can really throw."

The guy is 6-foot-5 Zach Mettenberger, a transfer from Georgia and Butler Community College, who is an upgrade from Jordan Jefferson, the LSU starter in the 2011 National Championship Game. Mettenberger, who grew up close to the UGA campus, got in some trouble at a Georgia bar and had to leave for Butler to get laundered, so to speak. He returned to the SEC as a third-string quarterback for LSU in 2011.

If he was so good, why didn't he supplant Jefferson as the starter in 2011? One reason was Miles's unfettered loyalty to Jefferson. The other reason is that not every JC quarterback is Cam Newton, who can bust out of a phone booth and produce a national championship.

There is LSU and, of course, there is Alabama, which is well greased with talent and can add to its national championship haul. The Crimson Tide made a reputation for great defensive lines the last several years, but the Bama offensive line the next two seasons will be the backbone of the team. The unit includes 2013 first-round pick Chance Warmack and left tackle D. J. Fluker.

It will take all of the strength of the SEC superpowers to hold off Southern Cal and Lane Kiffin, and Bob Stoops and Oklahoma, and Fisher and FSU in the next few seasons. Ohio State will soon fill up the SEC's rearview mirror. Michigan State has the look of a consistent top ten program. And can Texas, with its multitude of resources, continue to be so above average? The Longhorns should be great, and they're not. They are just above average, and you can scratch your head over that one all day long.

Texas A&M and Missouri joined the SEC on July 1, 2012. The Aggies wasted no time declaring their allegiance to the SEC. They adorned just about any flat space they could find with the SEC logo.

They vended the SEC to recruits, and it did them some good with commitments around their state with first-year coach Kevin Sumlin. You can hear the recruiting pitch: "Come play against the best."

The addition of Texas A&M would appear to give the SEC a wider recruiting door to talent-rich Texas. Taylor Hamm of GigEm-247Sports (tamu.247sports.com) said the SEC is already in Texas, so there won't be the recruiting bonanza so many people envision.

"LSU is already in Texas recruiting, so is Alabama," Hamm says. "Will Muschamp of Florida. Where did he just come from? Austin and UT. You think he doesn't already know his way around?"

The school that will benefit, Hamm said, is A&M. The Aggies slapped the SEC logo on the fence that surrounds their practice field and sewed the logo onto practice shirts and beamed with pride. A&M couldn't wait to join the glory and exposure and get some of the haul of TV money, and a chance to showcase the SEC to recruits.

"Only a few recruits have said it was a bad move for A&M," Hamm says. "More have said it is a chance to play in a great conference like the SEC and a chance to stay at home. Kevin Sumlin has had success recruiting and the SEC has helped him."

Here is what else is Next for the SEC . . . off the field.

There has to be a social policy change at SEC schools. Plain and simple, football players need to be made true members of the student body again. Some are, many are not. They are viewed as mercenaries, and it degrades the whole product the SEC puts on the field.

The faculty at SEC schools need to be more familiar with the athletes, which could stop some of the heckling from the rest of college football that the SEC just takes this winning thing too seriously. The conference can never sanitize itself enough for the Big

Ten, among others, because of the money the SEC is spending on football. But one reason the heckling has gotten louder is the faculty at SEC schools do not hide their displeasure with what is happening on campus with football. When professors get a chance to criticize football, they do it, usually with anonymous comments, but sometimes in the open.

Who can blame them? Players have systematically been removed from the rest of the campus with demands on their time, which the NCAA itself confirms is a full-time workweek. Players leave the coaches at 6:00 p.m., but many are right back doing more conditioning work on their own or watching game film after 8:00 p.m., and the coaches throw up their hands and say, "Hey, they want to get better on their own." The weight room door is kept unlocked as part of the brainwashing: work harder than anybody else and you will get to the NFL or, at the very least, you get to keep your year-to-year scholarship.

"The faculty needs to have better access to the Division I football player," said Dr. Richard Southall, the director of the University of North Carolina College Sport Research Institute (CSRI). "Players are leery of the faculty, and they do not know who to trust on campus. They come from different backgrounds than these faculty. They have been isolated from the university's academic advising system at some schools.

"There is tension between what has become a commercialized enterprise, which is the football, and the education enterprise. You are trying to make football look educational when it is not . . . the issue becomes being honest about what you are doing."

USA Today and the *New York Times* have reported that programs steer players toward professors and classes where the easy grades flow from an open spigot. Some SEC football players are too busy to develop relationships with professors and classmates, so they go where they are told and miss some valuable campus time. They think the endgame is the diploma. It's not.

"Getting a diploma doesn't mean you received an education," Southall said. Indeed, as *USA Today* has reported, athletes can be disappointed with the degrees they receive when employers ask the tough questions.

Everybody knows that football coaches at some schools can take students who would not normally qualify academically in through the back door of the admissions office. These "special admits" help schools generate revenue. Just think about the top thirty to thirty-five football players on an SEC roster. These kids, the really talented players, are generating millions of dollars for schools, which funds other sports on campus, with the exception of basketball at some schools. If you take away some of these thirty to thirty-five players, the football program may not click and win games and make money and pay for many things in the athletic department. Some of those thirty to thirty-five stars are special admits.

Let me repeat that. Thirty students on campus—the stars—prop up the whole enterprise. Take away enough of those athletes and the enterprise collapses. So what do you do with the few special admits? Do you really shut the doors to them and deny them access to major institutions? That is incomprehensible for two reasons. One, some of these students come from some of the worst public school systems in America. Why not give them access to tutors and teach some solid skills?

Two, football is a skill whether or not you want to believe it. The university is providing a platform for the player to improve athletically and then go out and make a living and share the fruits with his family. The computer science class is training the next IBM technician. For the top tier of players, the starting twenty-two in the SEC, the football field is training them, but they also have to do the required academic work. I know, this is not the academic model that was set up 100 to 150 years ago, but in reality highly skilled athletes with economic power are on campus. If these players get enough time to devote themselves to academics and the faculty recognize the effort, the two sides can coexist. Some of the disdain for the revenue-producing athlete would go away, but coaches do not always make it easy for athletes to go to school, especially during the season.

Southall does not want to demonize the head coach, but says, "They have grown up in this system. They have a hard time seeing beyond their own worldview."

Mike Johnson, the former Alabama offensive lineman, takes offense at this idea that coaches hold back players and that the big-time players do not have a conscience.

"There are some great kids coming out of our school," Johnson said. "Look at Mark Ingram during his Heisman celebration. He's thanking everybody at the university. You see a guy like Julio Jones, who is this all-American receiver. Well, he may be a better blocker than he is receiver because he had to block and sacrifice for us to be successful."

Alabama had twenty-two players on its 2011 national championship team who had already secured their degrees. LSU has had 139 players graduate under Miles in his first seven seasons, or twenty per season. In 2008, Florida had a league-record thirty-seven players on the All-SEC Academic Honor Roll. Goliath's money—plus the idiots such as Florida running back Chris Rainey, who threatened to harm a woman—obscure the success in the classroom of SEC football players.

Rainey brings us to the true policy change the SEC needs to

implement: erasing its criminal element. Jordan Jefferson, the LSU quarterback, was allowed to return to the football team and represent the university after a vicious bar fight before the 2011 season. Former Auburn player Antonio Goodwin was sentenced to fifteen years in prison for first-degree robbery. Several teammates from the Tigers' national championship team await trial. Florida's Rainey was allowed back in uniform after his threats against a former girlfriend. Three Tennessee football players were arrested in 2009 for attempted armed robbery. In 2008, a heavily recruited high school lineman reached his hand underneath the dress of a hostess on one official visit, and the interested SEC school stopped recruiting him, as it should have. Not that it mattered. Another SEC school was standing by with a scholarship offer. The school with the new offer didn't know about the player's act? Well, they should have been told. It could have been prosecuted as sexual assault. Georgia's star running back Isaiah Crowell was found with a concealed weapon with an altered serial number. It goes on and on.

Players who are seen on national television representing a university need to be held to a different standard. University presidents have abdicated the responsibility because they cannot withstand the pressure of their football coach or boosters. The SEC, of course, has no say in the discipline of players on campus. Besides, Commissioner Mike Slive works for the SEC presidents and does what they tell him to do, which is one reason why Auburn skated away on the Cam Newton saga. Georgia has shown some backbone with regard to booting miscreants out of its program or suspending them. That has gotten the Bulldogs a label as a harbor for bad actors, but my suspicion is there are just as many troublemakers at other schools and they have been allowed to skate away.

When do parents of full-time students on campus start asking hard questions of the administration about some of the players who are recruited by SEC football coaches?

How many instances of bullying by football players on campus have gone unreported?

The ultimate question that has to be asked of the SEC and other major college football conferences comes from Mike Oriard, the former Notre Dame player and retired professor at Oregon State:

Are the student-athletes receiving the tools and training to lead a middle-class life after they leave school?

The data needs to be accumulated to see if Mark Richt, Nick Saban, Les Miles, Will Muschamp, and the rest of the coaches in the SEC are doing the job to the best of their abilities.

"We no longer live in a time where some old booster is going to hire you," Oriard said. "It's a much more competitive and meritocratic world out there. If you can't perform in some job you are hired for, it's not going to last."

Many sportswriters and those bloggers who write from their mother's basement would be surprised if they walked on campus and followed around some SEC players. More players than you think go to class; they make an effort. Some don't, but many more attempt to do the work. It is hard to play football in the SEC and achieve academically. That's why SEC schools have to ramp up the hiring of learning specialists for athletic departments. Big-money football is here to stay, so some of this money needs to be used for learning specialists, which are being hired by other schools around the country. A list of schools that have hired learning specialists was published in the *Chronicle of Higher Education* in June 2012. Of the twenty-three Football Bowl Subdivision schools that have hired learning specialists for athletes, just three were SEC schools: Texas A&M, LSU, and Tennessee.

The Knight Commission wants athletes who are accepted to a school to better match the profile of the academic students who are admitted to that school. That's not fair. The University of Georgia has become so exclusive that it turns down in-state students who have a 3.2 grade point average and 1200 SAT. The Georgia standards would deny admission to athletes from the below-average high schools in the South, which are underfunded and do not serve their communities well. Could these students instead go to small colleges and junior colleges? Sure, they could, but those schools have fewer resources than the wealthy SEC schools for helping these students achieve academically. SEC schools are helping meet the needs of impoverished students who are athletes. Are the schools getting rich off these kids? Absolutely. But some good is coming from it. Athletes are on campus with a chance to break through academically for the first time in their lives.

As always, the buck stops with the school presidents, and for years they were no match for their constituencies—alumni, donors, politicians, fans—who demanded a winner. With the help of the Knight Commission, the presidents are trying again to set the agenda for college athletics, but it is not an easy thing. When one conference makes a proposal for reform, the other conferences—led by competitive coaches, not presidents—wonder how it will affect competition on the playing field.

"The hope was that by having the presidents set the agenda they would be able to maintain the appropriate balance between the resources going into athletics and the resources being devoted to growing and strengthening the educational mission of the university," said Amy Perko, the executive director of the Knight Commission. "There have been successes in terms of academic reform and accountability measures. The struggle has been how to better balance the growing financial resources that the popularity of college football has been able to generate at the top levels and channel that so there is a better balance with the academic side of the house."

The public's appetite for college football has created a significant imbalance. While football budgets grow and grow in the SEC, the gap between spending per athlete and spending per academic student gets wider. Everyone has wondered if the spending in college football could be sustained. So far, the answer is yes because the TV networks keep raising rights fees in response to the game's popularity.

Just look at the numbers again: the SEC, according to the Delta Cost Project study released by the Knight Commission, was spending $156,833 on an athlete in 2009. It was spending $13,471 per student in 2009. The SEC is the pacesetter in terms of expenditures.

The SEC's string of titles has more to do with money and less to do with cheating. This book doesn't talk much about the high jinks in recruiting or keeping players eligible. It happens. Some SEC coach is probably breaking, or at least bending, a rule right now. But I bet a coach in another conference is up to the same stuff, too. SEC players are taking gifts and know it's wrong. The SEC has been labeled shameless when it comes to football and the pursuit of wins and championships. It is viewed as the worst offender of the NCAA rulebook, far ahead of other conferences, which is not even close to being true.

"I think most people feel it is difficult to deal with; all conferences probably have their issues and problems," said Dr. G. David Gearhart, the chancellor of the University of Arkansas, about rule-breaking and the athletics-first mentality in Division I football. "Our schools have had some issues, but I don't think it is any more prevalent than it is in other conferences.

"We did form an academic consortium of provosts and we put some money into that program, and I think we're making an effort to say it's about honor and integrity and academic performance. That was a strong and good move. We talk a lot about what is the right thing in sports. We have done some things in the SEC that have been on the leading edge, and I have found the presidents and chancellors keyed in to doing what's right."

So we'll cut this both ways and straddle a fence. The message in this book is that SEC football is to be adored on some levels and deplored on others. Football gives money back to the academic side in the SEC, millions of dollars of it, which many fans do not realize. SEC football trains players to be disciplined and accept hard coaching, which can only help them in the business world. Football also wrings everything it can out of a player, who works forty hours a week at football, but also has to deal with the pressures of being a full-time student. SEC football uses students who are football players to enrich coaches, athletic department administrators, television executives, and sponsors, but it also helps pay for athletes in other sports to compete and travel the country. Ask the volleyball players if they really want to see the money choked out of SEC football.

You can look at the dozens of SEC players who get an NFL paycheck and label it "stimulus" because the players work that money back through the system. It's employment. You're not just talking about the players who are drafted and signed. You are talking about the dozens who get invited to camps as free agents, get on practice squads for a season, and get invited back the next season, and so on. According to the NFL, undrafted rookie free agents get their room and board paid for during training camp and $850 to $1,000 a week to practice with the team for at least five weeks. Some more players make the practice squad, which is season-long employment at around $80,000.

"There is a class system in some countries where people can never rise above the place where they were born," said Les Miles, the LSU coach. "They were always going to be lesser-thans. It has nothing to do with skill and talent. They just happened to be in the wrong class, the wrong side of the tracks.

"The point is an economy that is healthy, a social structure that is healthy, allows for a redistribution of income. Those people that don't have great income need to have the ability to access income with hard work and skill and talent and energy. Football is a skill and talent, and there are those who can access income through playing college football. It allows them to ascend beyond class and social barrier. This is what football does, irrespective of whether you are Jewish, Baptist, white, or black. Football removes the barrier. Football is hard work. That's our country."

The other issue we should have with college football, not just the SEC, is that athlete welfare always seems so secondary to the TV money. It is an easy point to prove. Just consider the Thursday-night football games, which ruin Friday classes for the players on the team that has to travel. Leaving campus on Wednesday, playing Thursday, then going to bed at 2:00 a.m. does not make a sharp-eyed student on Friday. Then consider the long-distance travel that has been forced on athletes with conference expansion and how many of these athletes have to take self-directed courses online to stay eligible. Conferences expanded to make more money for coaches and administrators and placed a burden on athletes, who are students.

The expansion race has conferences trying to out-slick one another year after year, either through expansion or TV deals. The Pac-12 wants more money than the Big 12, which wants more money than the SEC, which wants more money than the Big Ten, and they all want to make sure they leave nothing for the ACC or Big East. Protect thyself, screw everybody else. College football attempts to get $6 out of you when you only have $5 in your pocket, but it's that way all across organized athletics, from the NFL down.

Maybe the SEC's luck is about to run out, judging by the calamity of the off-season before the 2012 season. Bobby Petrino, the Arkansas coach, had put together the makings of a top five team for 2012, but he was tossed out of his job after being caught in an affair with an employee and then lying about it.

The SEC was raked with ill will by the Big Ten, which claimed former Florida coach Meyer had imported ruthless recruiting practices—SEC-style ruthlessness—into the Big Ten. He was recruiting players who had committed to schools, but had not signed their scholarship papers.

Auburn lost star running back Michael Dyer to discipline issues and had players in court on a variety of charges. Tennessee kicked a player out of the program for criminal behavior. Georgia players were drug-tested after spring break and failed.

To top it off, the father of an Alabama player kicked the rug, which shook the pedestal, which spilled the national championship trophy. It broke into pieces. SEC fans shrugged at this. They figured they would get another trophy by next season anyway, hoist their Solo cups holding celebratory drink, and resume their chant: "SEC, SEC, SEC." Seemed like a typical off-season to most, except for the broken trophy.

The final message? The Southeastern Conference has football factories, no question about it, but Mike Johnson of Alabama, an offensive lineman, and Jason Watkins of Florida, also an offensive lineman, said some football players all across the SEC can walk on the academic side of the campus with their heads up. Some players are led to easy majors by handlers, but many others mix it up with the "regular" students.

The SEC has grown into Goliath, but it has a conscience. You can see it from the outside looking in if you look hard enough and want to find it.

ACKNOWLEDGMENTS

A lot of skilled reporters could have written this book. Jon Solomon of the *Birmingham News* is one. Ron Higgins of the *Memphis Commercial Appeal* is another. Bob Holt in Little Rock, Mike Herndon and Tommy Hicks in Mobile, Glenn Guilbeau in Louisiana, Ron Morris in Columbia, John Adams in Knoxville, Mark Schlabach and Chris Low of ESPN, Matt Hayes of the *Sporting News,* Andy Staples of CNN/*SI*, Tony Barnhart of CBS, and Paul Finebaum are among the others who know the SEC inside out and could have made this book sing. They have covered the SEC, which is not easy because the radar is always up at Alabama, Auburn, Tennessee, and elsewhere. Players are taught from the first day on campus to guard their words and not trust anybody in the media. Ninety percent of the media who cover the SEC will tell you that unnecessary roadblocks are thrown up by coaches, all in the name of student privacy, which is garbage. If you cover the SEC regularly, you know what I'm talking about. If you make a fan of a particular SEC school angry at you, it's the same phone call the reporter before you received: "You're not from around here, are you?" I got it when I worked in Knoxville.

I could write this book because I am a mercenary, a freelancer. I had the time. The other reporters have full-time jobs, which means they have to do their job, and the job of the guy/gal who just got laid off, and look over their shoulder wondering if they will be the next to get dumped on the street.

This book is dedicated to the sportswriters and editors still losing their jobs.

I had some go-to guys for this book. Phil Savage, the executive director of the Senior Bowl in Mobile, and the analyst for Alabama football radio broadcasts, helped steer me when I asked the simple question "How does Alabama find players for its system?" Phil was an NFL general manager and a scout. He helped build the Baltimore Ravens into a Super Bowl championship team. He knows Nick Saban. He knows people who know Nick Saban. More important, Phil knows football, and his insight was invaluable.

Mike Clayton, the LSU Tiger and NFL wide receiver, was a big help for this book in several chapters, and so was Michael Bonnette, the sports information director at LSU. Les Miles gave me a lot of time and didn't mind looking back at 2007 with a big season bearing down on him in 2012. Greg McGarity, the Georgia athletic director, helped me see the importance of facilities to help drive SEC football. I am grateful to the NCAA for mandating that head coaches stay on campus thirty days after the end of spring ball. It helped me catch up with Urban Meyer. Then there was Gil Brandt, the former Dallas Cowboys executive and NFL.com analyst. He answered the phone and answered questions. He also sent me a great picture of himself, Nick Saban, and Mack Brown with Saban in a Texas sweatshirt (it was taken while Saban was with the Dolphins).

The Florida duo of Chris Leak and Ron Zook shared the story of Florida's being built into a powerhouse again after the Steve Spurrier era. Florida's media guy Steve McClain helped me track down the Zooker and Leak, who have stayed in contact with each other. Auburn offensive-line coach Jeff Grimes and former center Ryan Pugh gave me something else to write about the Tigers besides Cam Newton, who had one of the greatest seasons in the history of the sport. Charles Bloom of the SEC clarified the SEC's role in some reforms, even during the hectic weeks of early June with college football buzzing over a play-off format.

I started this book on April 7, 2012, and finished it June 8, 2012. This book was a two-minute drill, a hurry-up offense, and Karen Longino, the managing editor for Howard Books, handled it with poise. She steered me right to the finish and fought some battles for me along the way.

One of the good things about 2:30 a.m. hunched over a computer is that you have the house to yourself and the dog is too tired to demand outside time. Alexander kept his batting average above .350 without as much batting practice pitching from me, and Raymond graduated from high school just fine and filled up his summer with one freelance yard job after another. A mercenary just like his old man. Jessie still wouldn't do my laundry while I worked on this book, but she did my share of the dishes and continues to make me feel blessed every day.

A mercenary such as me doesn't get a great project like this often, and it was fun to have my own spin on things. None of it would have been possible without the Southeastern Conference fan, the real difference-maker between the SEC and the rest of college football. Grab your Solo cup and salute yourself for making Saturdays so much fun.